B-24 Liberator
Combat Photographs from the Mediterranean Theater of War

BOB LIVINGSTONE

KEY Books

HISTORIC MILITARY AIRCRAFT SERIES, VOLUME 33

Front cover image: B-24H 42-52728 *Life* of 830th Bomb Squadron (BS), 485th Bomb Group (BG), was photographed over the Alps showing unmistakable evidence of a (historic) major oil leak from #2 engine. '728 flew 110 missions between July 7, 1944 and June 22, 1945, after which it was salvaged as war weary.

Title page image: A 9th Air Force (AF) B-24D thunders down a North African runway in 1943 trailing a cloud of dust as an airman waves the crew goodbye from the up-wind side of the runway. Behind this aircraft another is just commencing its take-off, while a third waits for the dust to settle before entering the runway.

Back cover image: Douglas-built B-24J 42-51284 taxies past the photographer at Manduria, Italy. Originally intended as an 8th AF replacement (the 8th AF combat modifications of cockpit armor-plate and bubble navigator's window are evident), this aircraft went into storage as there was a "glut" of B-24s in the UK at this time (late July 1944) caused by the 3rd Bomb Division (BD) changing to the B-17 aircraft. It was transferred to 15th AF in December 1944 and joined 722nd BS, 450th BG, as #44. It later returned to the US, and in October 1945 it was again in storage, this time at Altus, Oklahoma.

Published by Key Books
An imprint of Key Publishing Ltd
PO Box 100
Stamford
Lincs PE9 1XQ

www.keypublishing.com

The right of Bob Livingstone to be identified as the author of this book has been asserted in accordance with the Copyright, Designs and Patents Act 1988 Sections 77 and 78.

Copyright © Bob Livingstone, 2023

ISBN 978 1 80282 719 4

All rights reserved. Reproduction in whole or in part in any form whatsoever or by any means is strictly prohibited without the prior permission of the Publisher.

Typeset by SJmagic DESIGN SERVICES, India.

A small flight of 451st BG B-24s is shown heading for Ploești over broken cumulus; they have climbed into drier air above a thin contrail cloud, which has been created by a larger group of aircraft ahead of them.

Introduction

For Britain and its Empire, World War Two began on September 3, 1939, and once its land forces were forced out of Europe at Dunkirk in June 1940, the battle switched to North Africa to protect British interests in the Suez Canal and Middle Eastern oil fields. British-built heavy bombers such as the Stirling and Halifax were not operational until early 1941 and the Lancaster was still under development, so the Desert War began with light twin-engined types such as the Blenheim, Hudson and Beaufort. Britain had ordered the B-24 Liberator from Consolidated, but the early B-24s were not combat-ready. They had little or no protective armour, no self-sealing fuel tanks and only light defensive armament. The lack of engine turbo-charging meant that maximum heights left them vulnerable to anti-aircraft fire and fighters. Most were used as transports and Atlantic patrols taking advantage of their long range.

The Liberator II (LB-30 in the United States Army Air Force [USAAF]) that followed was marginally improved so these were pressed into service in North Africa, in desperation, the day after Tobruk fell to General Rommel's Africa Corps on June 21, 1942. 159 Squadron and elements of 160 Squadron began operations, followed in 1943 by 178 Squadron. These were joined by a small force of Halifax bombers. Both 159 and 160 Squadrons had originally been destined for India, and by March 1943 had left the Mediterranean theatre.

The USAAF entered the theater when the B-24D-equipped Halverson Detachment (HALPRO), intended to transit the area en route to airfields in China ready to begin attacks on Japan, but was caught up in North Africa, and instead of its intended destination was rushed into an attack, in early June 1942, on the Ploești oil fields in Romania. Penny-packet raids like this did nothing but alert the Germans to Ploești's vulnerability and gave them plenty of time to shore up defences, which later successfully hampered Allied attempts to shut the refineries down.

A trickle of replacement B-24s built the unit up again after combat attrition and in mid-July, by merging with the 9th Bomb Squadron (BS) of the 7th Air Force (AF), the two units became the 1st Bomb Group (Provisional) as the nucleus of the new US Army Middle East Air Force (MEAF) under the command of Maj. Gen. Lewis Brereton. The 98th Bomb Group (BG) joined them soon after. When the MEAF became the 9th AF, which began operations in November 1942, the 1st BG became the 376th BG.

Operation *Torch*, the November 1942 US invasion of Northwest Africa across three points on the Atlantic and Mediterranean coasts, brought in the 12th AF from the UK as the air support, which brought with it mainly fighters and medium bombers and four groups of B-17 bombers. During the B-24's assignments to the 9th and 12th AFs, their role was taking the offensive to the enemy, targeting shipping and harbour installations in Libya, Tunisia, Sicily, Italy, Crete and Greece, as well as road, rail and airfield transport facilities in Sicily and Italy. Both received Distinguished Unit Citations for *Tidal Wave* (see below) and their African-based operations.

One of the most famous USAAF bombing missions of World War Two happened on August 1, 1943, and is known as Operation *Tidal Wave*. It saw massed low-level B-24s attack oilfields in the vicinity of Ploești, Romania, from airfields around Benghazi in North Africa. The two 9th AF B-24 bomb groups were joined by the majority of three of the 8th AF's B-24 groups for the attack. As the "senior" members, the 9th AF groups each led separate formations of *Tidal Wave*. In total, 181 aircraft were rostered,

14 aborted, one crashed shortly after take-off, 53 further aircraft were lost to all causes, 306 men were killed, 139 made prisoners of war (POW) and 69 were interned. This was the greatest single-day loss of B-24s during World War Two across all theaters of operation.

In late August, the 8th AF, which was based in the UK, began a restructure, and the 9th AF began to transfer its assets, which included the 98th and 376th BGs, to the 12th AF to permit Brereton to take the 9th AF's command nucleus to the UK to become a tactical command unit in the lead-up to D-Day. This structure only lasted for a short time, as by November 1943 the 12th's heavy bombers, both B-17s and B-24s, began to transfer to the new 15th AF and move to Italy.

The movement of the 15th AF eastward to Bari was enabled by the Italian campaign liberating the southern portion of the country, and as more B-24 groups were formed in the US, it grew to be the largest operator of the B-24 in the Mediterranean Theater of Operations (MTO), growing from four to 15 heavy bomb groups of the type, intended to, as Winston Churchill put it, attack Germany and German-occupied territories through Europe's "soft underbelly." It also fielded six B-17 groups. The highest category targets for these AFs throughout World War Two were the German-controlled oil producing and refining locations, particularly Ploești in Romania.

NOTE: 15th AF quickly became a large operation. In addition to the 21 heavy bomber groups, it fielded seven fighter groups (equipped with P-38, P-47 and P-51), a reconnaissance group and three squadrons of specialist aircraft, mainly B-24s. A system of bright colors and designs painted on the bombers' tails was devised to identify each bomb group, and large colored numbers or letters were painted on individual squadron aircraft to identify them, particularly in flight, and were used as radio call signs. Four B-24 bomb wings (11 groups) used numbers and one (four groups) used letters. In the captions to the photographs that follow, the aircraft identifying number is written in a consistent style, eg #31, and the letters in their phonetic alphabet style, eg, B-Baker. Adding the colors would make the text complex.

An effort has been made to include images of as many as possible of these protagonists in the B-24's Mediterranean Theater of War (MTO).

A mixed flight of 15th Air Force (AF) B-24s and B-17s heads north over the Alps in early summer 1944, bound for a target in Southern Germany. In the foreground is B-24H 42-99858 *Dopey*, the fourth squadron aircraft to be so named, up from its 343rd Bomb Squadron (BS), 98th Bomb Group (BG), base at Lecce, Italy. This aircraft was lost on August 18, 1944, on a Ploești, Romania, mission when under the command of 1st Lt. Raymond L. Baker. Unable to maintain height with engines No.1 and No.2 out and unable to be feathered, the crew had to bale out. All but the nose gunner, Pvt. John O. White, Jr., who refused to jump and was killed when the aircraft crashed, became prisoners of war (POW).

Not long after dawn on August 1, 1943, B-24D 42-40664 *Teggie Ann*, #100, taxies out at Benghazi, Libya, for departure on Operation *Tidal Wave* — the massed low-level B-24 attack on the Ploești oilfields — under the command of the 376th BG Commanding Officer, Lt. General K. K. Compton and accompanied by the Ploești Mission Commander, General Uzal Ent. Partially obscured by dust, B-24D 41-24033, #81, of 515th BS, piloted by 1/Lt. Charles W. Bley, prepares to follow. Both aircraft returned from the hell of Ploești, but '033 crashed on November 5, 1943, and '664 was shot down by flak over Melfi, Italy, on August 16, 1943.

Ford-built B-24J 42-50591 of 718th BS, 449th BG, is shown at Grottaglie, Italy, after suffering a common B-24 failure — a nosewheel collapse. Accepted by the Army Air Forces (AAF) in April 1944, it arrived at Bari, Southern Italy, on July 7 to be assigned to the 449th BG. While the date of the incident is not known, it is likely to have been in October 1944, as it was returned to the 718th BS on November 19. '591, although modified as a PB-24 Pathfinder, does not carry the overall neutral gray paintwork usually carried by 15th AF PB-24s. At the end of European hostilities, '591 was returned to the US, and by October 1945 was parked among the many other unwanted warplanes at Altus, Oklahoma.

Despite a distinct lack of information on this aircraft's career, B-24H-DT 41-28990 (a Douglas Tulsa product) was accepted by the Army Air Force (AAF) in February 1944. It entered combat with 720th BS, 450th BG, in mid-May, but in September it suffered a nose-wheel collapse and was salvaged.

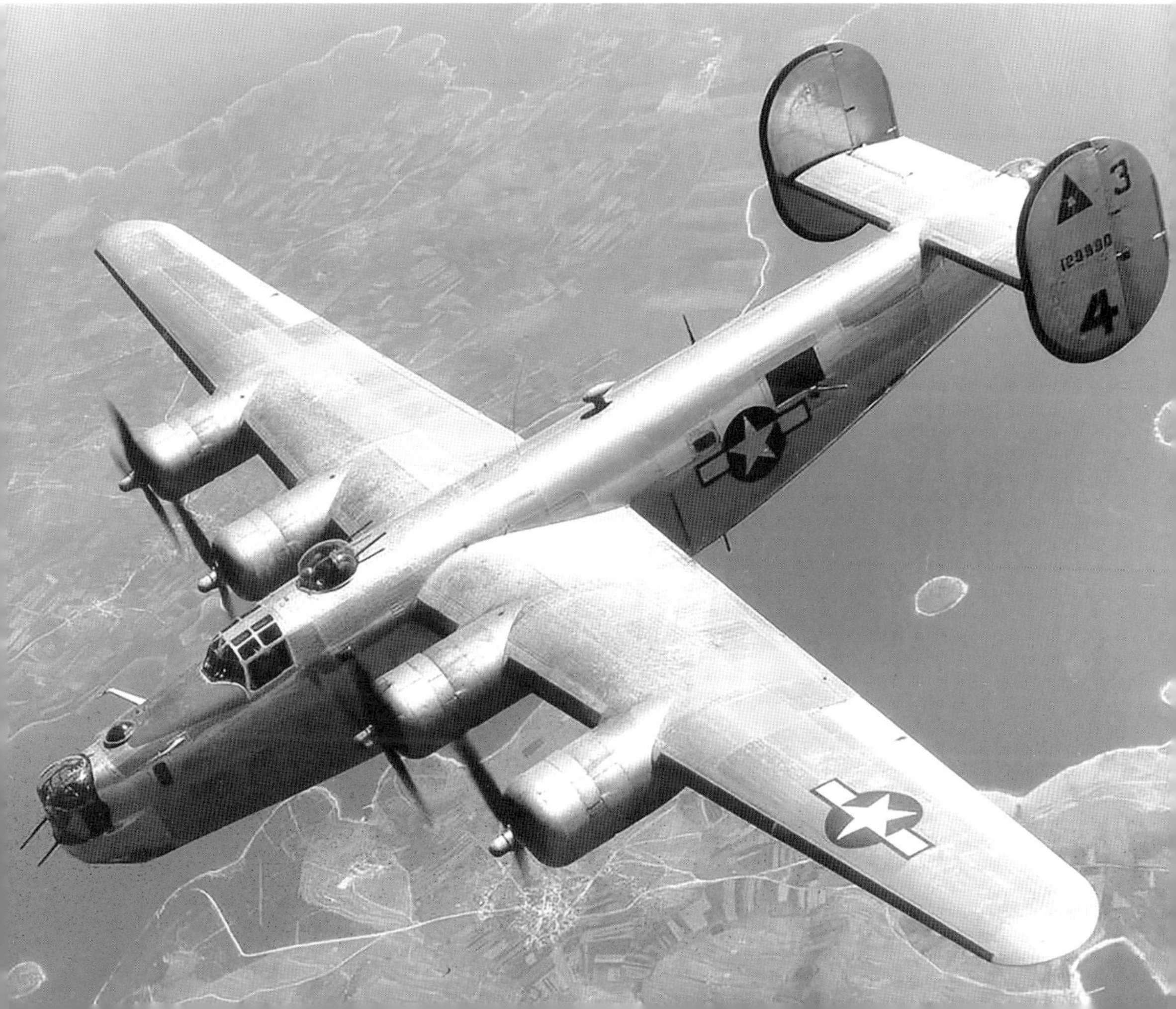

Although accepted by the AAF on July 5, 1944, it was not until September 26 that B-24J-FO 42-51674 departed for the combat area, the delay being caused by a six-week hold for modification to Pathfinder standard. On arrival in Italy, it was further modified to suit local conditions, including painting in neutral gray, a 15th AF requirement for Pathfinders. It was not until October 19 that it was received by 727th BS, 451st BG, for operations. The photo shows it after a nosewheel collapse on March 7, 1945; note the A-3D "high-hat" turret for the lead-computing K-8 gunsight. It was quickly repaired, and in May it was sent to Gioia del Colle (the major 15th AF depot) and from there to Grenier Air Force Base (AFB) in the US for storage. After six months it was obvious that its specialities would no longer be needed, and on January 12, 1946, it was sent to Walnut Ridge, Arkansas, to await salvage.

B-24G-NT 42-78458 of 737th BS, 454th BG, is interned at Dübendorf near Zurich, Switzerland, waiting out its internment during the war. Un-named '458, under the command of 1/Lt. Thomas P. Faulkner, had diverted there after engines #2 and #3 were shot out by flak during the 454th's mission number 202, an attack on rail marshalling yards at Augsburg, Germany, on February 27, 1945. The nine crewmen were interned "for the duration" and the aircraft was flown back to the UK on September 22, 1945, after being made airworthy again. That was likely its last flight, as it is recorded as salvaged under the code FEA (From Enemy Action) exactly one month later.

The crew of Lt. Winton S. Reynolds poses beside the aircraft it took to war; B-24G 42-78470 *Windy Clipper* is pictured with art designed and painted on the aircraft by Reynolds. The crew was assigned to 722nd BS, 455th BG, and flew its first mission on July 25, 1944, to the Hermann Göring Steel Works at Linz, Austria. On its second mission to Budapest, Hungary, on July 27, 1944, it was shot up badly, with two engines out and with the hydraulic system inoperative. After the emergency landing, *Windy Clipper* never really flew properly again and was sent to Gioia, Italy, in December 1944 for inspection and correction, after which it was reportedly sent to 456th BG and later salvaged on February 13, 1945.

A formation of 774th BS B-24s of 456th BG cruise over the Adriatic, bound from their base at Stornara, Italy, for a target in Austria. The nearest aircraft is B-24G 42-78418 *The Blonde Bomber*. On December 19, 1944, '418's ten crew, led by 2/Lt. William H. Lyman Jr., was lost when it crashed into a hillside near Deira Corvi, Italy. It was suspected to have been damaged by flak over the target — a marshalling yard at Graz — and was last seen disappearing into a cloud layer after lagging behind the main formation during the return to base.

Appearing as a fearsome monster, PB-24H-DT 41-28802 from the 756th BS, 459th BG, awaits a taxi clearance with engines ticking over. Originally known as *Satan's Shuttlebus*, this gray-painted Pathfinder was combat-damaged in the nose so it was sheeted over and repainted as *The Yellow Nosed Monster*. Unlikely to be used in combat like this, it probably became a squadron or group hack and is known to have been ferried back to the US in June 1945, and received at Altus, Oklahoma, on July 28, 1945, for sale by the Reconstruction Finance Company.

B-24J-FO 42-51916 reached 15th AF on August 29, 1944, and after processing became a replacement assigned to 763rd BS, 460th BG, as K-King on September 20, 1944. The photo shows the aircraft without any of the 460th BG markings, so it must be very early after arrival. Between February 28, 1945, and March 31, it underwent a major service at Gioia, but returned to the 763rd until the end of the European war. It returned to the US and was sent to Hill Field in northern Utah for storage on June 16, 1945, where it was later salvaged.

#22, B-24H-DT 41-28927 of 765th BS, 461st BG, did not last long enough to receive a name. Accepted on February 17, 1944, and departed for Italy on March 1, it was received by 15th AF on March 9. The crew photograph with the new aircraft was taken on April 19. When the squadron aircraft were being readied for the day's mission on May 8, 41-29367, Lady Bird, #32, caught fire and the bomb load exploded. Five aircraft from the 765th, including 41-28927 were damaged Category 5 and written off. The "519" on the nose was the Douglas airframe construction number.

This Pathfinder B-24H-DT (note the radar dome where the ball turret usually appears) wearing the markings of 464th BG but without any visible serial number; a not uncommon feature of 15th AF aircraft. Often the factory-applied serial number was on the outward face of the vertical stabilizer and when the Group markings were applied, the serial was overpainted and not replaced. This is 42-51136, T-Tare, of 776th BS, an unlucky aircraft that was shot down by flak on its first mission to Ploești (on July 22, 1944), under the command of Major Harold E. Blehm and crashed with only four survivors at Pazardzhik, Bulgaria.

An often published but not often identified photograph of Pathfinder B-24H-DT 41-28853, I-Item, 783rd BS, 465th BG, begins its plunge to earth after taking a direct hit in the fuel tank between #3 engine and the fuselage. The aircraft was hit over the target, the Blechhammer-South oil refinery in Poland, and the pilot, 781st BS Commanding Officer (CO) and 55th Bomb Wing leader Lt. Col. Clarence "Jack" Lokker survived, to be killed on the ground. Six others became POWs.

This grainy image, a portion of a much larger original image, shows the aircraft a few seconds later having shed its right wing, which can be seen on the far-left edge of the frame.

Details are limited on this accident. What is known is that it is 41-29507 #22 of 824th BS, 484th BG, and that it crashed at Torretta, Sicily, on October 8, 1944, after six months of combat operations with the 824th BS. The condition of the wreckage shows unmistakable damage caused by a stall—little forward vector movement but a large vertical vector. The location is the aircraft's home base, suggesting that it is a take-off or landing accident. If it was on take-off for a mission, I would expect to see major crash evidence and fire, so it seems it may have been a landing accident, possibly fuel starvation and a stall caused by attempting to "stretch the glide" to the runway.

Beast face or dragon face? B-24J-FO 42-50899 of 828th BS, 485th BG, carried no name, just the art. There is conflicting information about the fate of this aircraft. During a mission on November 11, 1944, a radio operator described hearing this aircraft reporting the loss of two engines and an attempt to make Falconara, on the Adriatic, in an emergency landing, while another reported that the crew had baled out over Yugoslavia. No records can be found to support these reports — no accident report, no Missing Aircrew Report (MACR). The aircraft card carries a write-off date of December 9, 1944, due to a taxi accident at home base Venosa, so somehow it made it back to base.

Royal Air Force (RAF) Liberator II AL550, M-Mike (and thus named *Monica Drops Them*), of 159 Squadron being attended to in a revetment at St Jean, Palestine, in 1942; the vertical stabilizer shows evidence of flak damage from the evening before. On April 27, 1943, this aircraft crashed into an aircraft shelter at Salbani with no brake pressure, causing serious damage, and was subsequently passed to 1584 Heavy Conversion unit after a lengthy repair. It was finally lost on September 8, 1944, after ditching off Sharjah after engine failure. (Photo courtesy of Matt Poole)

Two very late war deliveries to 415th BS, 98th BG, cruise in formation. The nearest is B-24M-FO 44-50483, L-Love, and the other is B-24J-FO 42-50913, B-Baker. Both were originally intended as 8th AF replacements but transferred to the 15th AF as "surplus to requirements." '913 was the first to arrive on January 20, 1945, and flew missions from January 31 until the 98th was taken off operations on April 15, 1945, subsequently being returned to the US on June 28 and stored at Altus, Oklahoma. '483 arrived on February 25, 1945, and flew missions from March 1, returning to the US and received at Kingman, Arizona, for storage on December 6, 1945.

A flight of 513th BS, 376th BG, B-24s over the foothills of the Alps heads for the target. Of the five aircraft, the two with the natural metal finish are identified. Highest is 42-50421, #53/L, and lowest is 44-40490, #46/C, *No No Cleo*. '421 was lost on July 27, 1944, when it crashed on take-off and '490 was damaged by flak on October 17, 1944, and crash-landed at 456th BG base, Stornara, on the return flight.

This photo is not all that it appears to be. On March 29, 1944, 42-52106 *Sunshine*, #05, of 719th BS, 449th BG, was the tail-end aircraft in the formation en route to attack the marshalling yards at Bolzano, near the Swiss and Austrian borders in northern Italy. One engine failed, and losing height and speed, it turned for Switzerland and jettisoned its bombs. Flak took out another engine and it force-landed at German-occupied Venegono, Italy. After interrogation, the crew were filmed disembarking from the aircraft for German propaganda. Nose gunner Mal Harper kept flashing the V-sign to ruin the film, but it was edited out. The crew went to Stalag Luft I and *Sunshine* was flown by KG200 as FL+HL until shot down by German flak on April 6, 1945, during a ferry flight from Hildesheim to Bavaria.

During the 450th BG mission on February 22, 1944, radar B-24H-FO 42-7760 of 722nd BS had its nosewheel shot away and crash-landed on the runway on return. The pilot, 2/Lt. Willis R. Retzlaff was commended for his skill as he had two wounded aboard, tail gunner Sgt. Melvin C. Hellem and waist gunner Sgt. Walter S. Johnson. Not readily visible in the photo, but the action around the nose turret is because the nose gunner, whose name unfortunately was not recorded, was trapped inside.

This was the scene at Castelluccio when B-24J-FO 42-51679 of 726th BS, 451st BG, had the #2 propeller run away during take-off. It went off the runway into a ditch and caught fire as the crew scrambled out. The day's mission was cancelled and the other aircraft shut down on the taxiway, waiting for the bombs to explode, which took almost an hour. One engine was thrown completely through the rear fuselage of a B-24 having a wheel changed and knocked it off its jack stand, and one propeller was found over half a mile away. The #23 visible is 41-29256 *Sakinshack,* of 724th BS, still on its hardstand.

B-24L-FO 44-49841, #64, of 738th BS, 454th BG, has just released its first bombs over Krems on April 2, 1945. It was assigned to the squadron on February 3, 1945, and flew missions until the 15th AF was stood-down on May 1, 1945. On June 16, it was ferried back to the US for storage at Greenville, South Carolina, because it was such a late-model B-24. With so many new aircraft having gone from factory direct to storage, it was "revived" on January 14, 1946, and flown to Walnut Ridge for salvage.

The sight of this burning wreckage would not have been welcomed by the tired crews in the aircraft seen above. B-24H-FO 42-94982 of 743rd BS, 455th BG, was badly damaged by fighter attacks during the April 20, 1944, mission to the shipyards at Monfalcone, Italy. Upon landing at San Giovanni, the pilot, 2Lt. Robert L. Cook, was unable to prevent it veering off the runway and crashing into a gasoline truck. However, the crew managed to escape before the aircraft was destroyed. It is recorded that Charles Lindberg, a Colonel in the USAAF, performed the 2.5-hour acceptance checks on this aircraft at the factory before AAF acceptance on February 25, 1944.

Another late model B-24L-FO, 44-49453 *Baby Boots*, M-Mike, of 746th BS, 456th BG, is the backdrop for this experienced crew. Delivered from the factory to the AAF on October 21, 1944, '453 reached the 746th BS on February 18, 1945, ending its combat career at the end of April. It returned to the US for storage and salvage at Walnut Ridge, Arkansas, on January 4, 1946.

This pile of junk is half of what remained of B-24J-CF 44-10565 of 767th BS, 459th BG, after taking a direct hit from anti-aircraft (AA) after passing over the target — Blechammer — on August 22, 1944. Control was immediately lost and the pilot, 2/Lt. Wendell G. Garrett, ordered everyone to bale out. Everyone except the bombardier, 2/Lt. Leon P. Cook, who landed on electricity wires suffering burns and then a fall to the ground, made it down safely. A crewman in another aircraft described seeing the aircraft hit the ground in a huge cloud of dust without fire or explosion. All crew, after nine months as POWs, returned to the US in May 1945.

With #2 propeller feathered, major oil loss and the photographic aircraft above casting its shadow on it, B-24H-FO 42-52370, X-X-ray, of 763rd BS, 460th BG, heads home to Spinazzola at reduced speed. The emblem on the nose is the 460th's black panther identifier. '370 was one of the Group's originally assigned aircraft when it was formed in the US in July 1943 and is believed to have been named *Pack Rat*. '370 was written off on July 13, 1944.

This is what is known in the military as "hurry up and wait." A line up of 461st BG aircraft wait for the order to take off. Being refuelled from a 55-gallon drum is B-24J-DT 42-51306, #15, of 767th BS. Later transferred to 725th BS, 451st BG, it was shot down on December 2, 1944, by AA over Blechammer, and was seen by the pilots of the aircraft following to suddenly bank sharply left and dive out of sight. The navigator was either killed or badly wounded and was dropped from the nosewheel opening and his ripcord pulled. The co-pilot, who was believed to speak Polish, was thought to have been killed on the ground while trying to avoid capture. The remainder of the crew became POWs and returned to the US in June and July 1945.

Streaming fuel from a flak-holed tank on the left wing, B-24G 42-78472, C-Charlie, of the 777th BS, 464th BG, diverted to Gioia for repair on October 17, 1944. It returned to the squadron on November 16, only to suffer a landing accident when returning from a practice mission on December 4 when the nose gear collapsed. Damage included three bulkheads slightly bent, and damage to the nose section. After another repair, it was back on line on April 20, 1945, returning to the US on May 30 and to Altus, Oklahoma, on October 19 for storage and salvage.

B-24J-FO 42-51996, L-Love, of 783rd BS, 465th BG, explodes and begins to disintegrate at 26,000ft over Munich on November 16, 1944, after a direct AA hit in the left wing-root only a few seconds from bombs away; bombs can be seen being flung out of the bomb bay. The pilot, Capt. Irving R. Stringham, and co-pilot, 2/Lt. Delbert C. Brimhall, had just stood up and taken off their flak jackets. Brimhall was blown from the cockpit but survived; the pilot was never seen again. The navigator, 2/Lt Eugene M. Kipp, was also blown out and survived. The remaining members of the crew were all either killed in the explosion or trapped by the centrifugal force exerted by the out-of-control aircraft spinning down.

Not a happy ending for what had been a successful practice mission. 2Lt. Charles E. Nash and a limited crew flew B-24G 42-78364, #51, of 826th BS, 484th BG, on a three-hour bombing and gunnery mission on June 27, 1944, and after landing, taxied back to the revetment. Part way through the turn into the bay, the right main gear collapsed, causing write-off damage: #3 and #4 propellers and engines, right landing gear, wing and bomb bay doors, front pivot shaft, bulkhead, catwalk and fuselage skins. An inspection determined that Nash's landing had been normal in every respect, and that the structure had been weakened by a previous and unreported heavy landing, and that routine inspections had failed to detect the damage.

Looking rather unloved, B-24H-FO 42-52729 of 829th BS, 485th BG, lies on the Island of Vis, where it had been pushed out of the way and abandoned after an emergency landing on September 5, 1944. There is evidence that parts of the aircraft have been stripped to assist the repair of other aircraft. Prior to this, the only noteworthy incident for this aircraft had been a precautionary landing at Zara, Yugoslavia, to add fuel before continuing back to base in Italy. Vis was a very important emergency landing point not far from the coast of Croatia, before the long haul across the Adriatic back to the Southern Italy bomber bases. It was here where the AAF maintained a small repair crew to patch up damaged aircraft. Not all made it, and the ocean floor around the island is littered with B-24 wrecks, which today are being dived on by local aircraft archaeologists.

Liberator II AL574, O-Orange, of RAF 108 Squadron at Fayid, Egypt, in early December 1941. This aircraft had been flown direct from Bolling Field, Washington, to the Middle East, piloted by USAAF pilot David B. Lancaster, arriving on December 9. On December 18, it departed Fayid for Palembang, Sumatra, under the command of Squadron Leader K. F. Vare, carrying a quantity of Blenheim IV spares for 84 Squadron, which had recently been dispatched from the Middle East to the war in the Indies, taking 57.5 flying hours for the 12,000-mile round trip. Note that it does not carry an upper turret. On February 22, 1942, pilot officer F. H. McDonald took off for a reconnaissance mission from Fayid at 02 30hrs, retracted the undercarriage too soon, crashed and the aircraft burned. The crew escaped serious injury.

In late September 1943, the 376th BG moved to Enfidaville, Tunisia, and its first mission from there was an attack on Wiener Neustadt on October 1. Group CO, Col. Compton, led Section A, and Major Forrest in B-24D 42-72927 led Section B. The weather was overcast and bombing results were unable to be observed. On the way home, after descending to 9,000ft, the formation was unexpectedly fired upon by flak guns near the Italian city of Campobasso, and '927 as lead aircraft was hit numerous times. Knox, his co-pilot (Crosby) and the navigator (Hennel) were seriously wounded and the bombardier (Tomashosky) killed. An RAF observer (Powell) assisted the wounded co-pilot to get to Tunis, where the aircraft ran out of fuel overhead the field and crash-landed.

716th BS, 449th BG B-24J-FO 42-51477 #63 drops a load of fragmentation bombs and incendiaries on the target. On April 17, 1945, while providing infantry support over Bologna, on almost the last of 254 missions for the 449th BG, '477 had two engines knocked out by flak and limped on with 2/Lt. Kenneth D. Parkins at the controls to crash land at Pontedera in Tuscany. The nose and left main gear collapsed and the aircraft was written off.

B-24J-DT 42-51175, #72, of 723rd BS, 450th BG, burns on the taxiway beside the runway at Manduria. During the take-off roll, the #2 engine exploded and shed the propeller, with flames reaching past the waist windows. Pilot 2/Lt. Richard D. Seeman steered the aircraft off the runway on to the taxiway and brought it to a halt. In this short time, a large fire had broken out. Four NCO crew escaped with minor injuries, but the nose gunner was killed, as were all officer crew including pilot, co-pilot and navigator. Within six minutes of the fire starting, 2,700 gallons of fuel and 4,000lbs of bombs exploded.

These are the last moments of B-24J-FO 42-51729, #28, of 724th BS, 451st BG, after being attacked by a formation of German fighters over Markersdorf, Austria, on August 23, 1944. Engines #3 and #4 burst into flames and the aircraft went into a spin. After falling about 3,000ft, the right wing separated from the fuselage and the tail gunner in another aircraft sighted four parachutes. In the photo, the wing and both engines can be seen falling separately. The pilot, 2/Lt. Robert L Beach, and all other crew escaped from the aircraft, though the co-pilot and nose gunner were suspected to have been killed by civilians on the ground. The others became POWs and returned to the US after the end of the war.

B-24H-FO 42-52205, Bama Baby, #32, was original equipment belonging to 739th BS, 454th BG, but transferred in June 1944 to 718th BS, 449th BG, with which it flew 29 missions until October 13 when it landed at Tortorella rather than home base Grottaglie, most likely with combat damage. It never returned to 449th BG, becoming one of the small number of USAAF B-24s selected to operate on Detached Service with 301 Squadron RAF on clandestine night flights, where it became RAF serial number TW759 as a Liberator B.VI. When returned to the AAF, it was declared war weary and salvaged at Bari on February 13, 1945.

A very clear, sharp image of a brand-new B-24 on a factory test flight. This B-24J-CF was destined to operate with 742nd BS, 455th BG, as *What's Cookin' Doc?* #46. On August 17, 1944, the aircraft was shot down by AA fire at Ploești after receiving a direct flak hit on #3 engine. It burst into flames, went into a dive and after about 5,000ft the tail broke off. Three crew were killed, including one whose parachute caught fire immediately after it opened.

This rather battered aircraft was B-24J-FO 42-52304 *Barbara Jane* of 745th BS, 456th BG, which later passed to 747th BS, with which it suffered a take-off accident at Stornara on January 21, 1945, when piloted by 2/Lt. James F. Jackson. All crew survived.

B-24J-FO 42-52359 *Aces Over*, has gathered a group of interested soldiers. The 757th BS of the 459th BG attacked Viterbo Main with 310 500-pounders on March 7, 1944, with good results. An oil dump and hangar were hit, but two aircraft were lost to moderate flak, and '359 came down in a forced landing in the Naples area. Damage and the isolated location meant that the aircraft was stripped of useful parts and written off.

B-24J-FO 42-52420, D-Dog of 762nd BS, 460th BG, shows off its complex early 15th AF identification markings, though the silhouette of a black panther has yet to be added to the white patch on the nose. For some reason, it was transferred to the 783rd BS, 465th BG, to become L-Love. On July 8, 1944, the flak-damaged aircraft left Vienna heading toward Hungary. The crew baled out near Kemenesszentpéter. The empty aircraft kept descending and hit the ground near Külsővat, where it exploded on impact. The flying debris hit two men (father and son) working in the fields who were both killed. The Royal Hungarian Police reported 20 captured American airmen at nearby Magyargencs — including some of this crew.

On March 31, 1945, B-24J-FO 42-51838, *Natural*, #65, of 767th BS, 461st BG, seen here flying in company with the Squadron's P-40F *Mary C*, were returning from a mission when, in the words of Cpl. Denver Hamm, Jr., "Lt. Connor's ship caught prop wash from the ships in number two position, and apparently he lost control of the plane, for it went into a very steep bank through the formation and was going down quite fast with his left wing low when he went into the clouds." The formation was over the Adriatic at the time, and '838 is assumed to have crashed into the ocean with all crew lost.

About 30 minutes after leaving the target (rail marshalling yards in Munich) on November 14, 1944, two turbos went out, and this, combined with one engine running away and the propeller unable to be feathered about an hour previously, meant that the aircraft was unable to maintain height. After the aircraft had descended through the undercast, all crew baled out on command and all were captured, becoming POWs. The aircraft was B-24J-CO 44-41084, L-Love, of 778th BS, 464th BG, and was seen by one of the crew to fly into the side of a mountain and explode.

2/Lt. James Winton Griffith and his 781st BS crew were tasked with 465th BG bombing mission #123 to the railroad yards at Maribor, Yugoslavia, on December 19, 1944, flying 783rd BS's B-24J-CO 44-41106, N-Nan. At approximately 13 25hrs, they suffered engine failure at 25,000ft over Lake Balaton, Hungary. Lt. Griffith gave orders to bale out, but only six crewmen were able to escape through the bomb bay before the aircraft crashed into the lake. Griffith and three others died in the crash. Two bodies, including Griffith's, washed ashore near a small Hungarian town and were subsequentially buried in a nearby churchyard by local people. The other two crew members are still listed as missing. Sgt. Carlson was wounded and spent several days in two different Hungarian hospitals before being turned over to German authorities.

"A hunting we will go!" One of the earliest USAAF B-24s to begin operations from North Africa is this Halverson Project (HALPRO) B-24D, 41-11597, #19, named *Blue Goose*. It was named as such by its original pilot, A. W. Moore, "because of its blue bottom and because the wild goose flies high and far." B-24Ds with serial numbers 41-11588 to 41-11671, originally contracted to the RAF, were painted in the RAF High Altitude Bomber Scheme — with base surfaces deep sky blue (Duco No.71-052) — 46 of which were appropriated by the USAAF when the US entered the war. *Blue Goose* flew on the HALPRO Ploești mission of June 12, 1942, and was one of the aircraft interned in Turkey due to two flak-damaged engines. Note the camera port modification in the nose. It is believed that this aircraft became #4003 in the 2nd Batt./3rd Company until late 1946, equipped as a special long-range transport for the Chief of the Turkish Armed Forces.

B-24D 41-11895 was assigned to 98th BG, 343rd BS, and named *Blond Bomber*. It only ever flew one operational mission — on August 29, 1942, before crashing on a training flight on September 1. It was patched up and arrived at Gura, Eritrea, on November 25, where the USAAF maintained a major depot and repair station. Its history after repair is murky, but it did not return to the 98th BG, and is believed to have been sent to the 7th BG for use as a hack and renamed *Pinky the Pimp* because of its "desert pink" paintwork. It was not written off until April 2, 1945.

"We must stop meeting like this!" B-24J-CO 44-40149, *Babs,* #77, was not a lucky aircraft. Arriving at the 514th BS, 376th BG, on April 19, 1944, it soon suffered a nosewheel collapse. After repair, it had a brake failure while being taxied and ran into 42-52557, #66, on May 18. It was repaired by replacing the nose turret from a painted aircraft and renamed *Bull Moose*. Apparently, there were further problems and after being sent to Gioia, it returned to the BG as a war-weary hack, stripped of all armament and turrets. Notwithstanding its status, it flew on the 15th AF maximum mission of April 15, 1945. According to one squadron veteran, "as soon as she had completed the bomb run, she peeled off and made a bee-line home." With all the equipment removed, maybe it was much faster than the others. It was salvaged at Gioia not long afterwards.

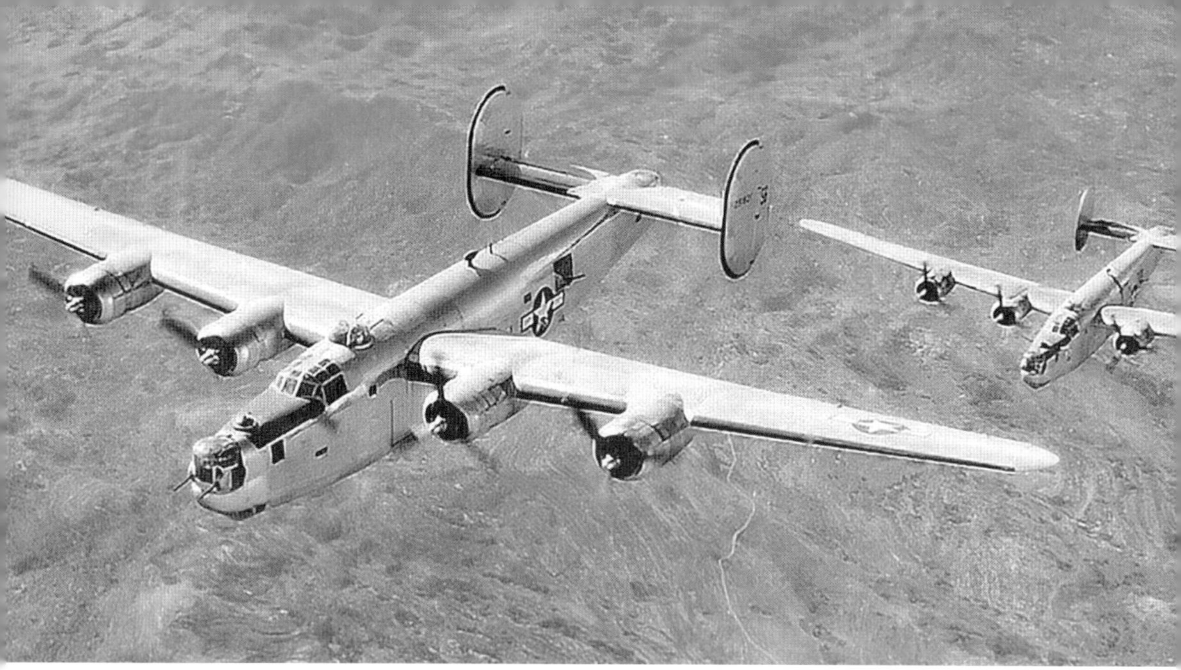

B-24J-FO 42-51821, #56, of 717th BS, 449th BG. Accepted at Willow Run by the USAAF on July 17, 1944, the aircraft proceeded through the usual channels being ferried by Air Transport Command (ATC) to Hamilton AFB, California, to be assigned a combat crew to fly it to the combat zone. When matched with a suitable crew, it departed for Italy on August 25 and arrived at Bari after a slow trip on September 12 to be pooled until needed as a replacement, which happened on October 20. Here the crew was assigned a combat unit on arrival and almost certainly never saw the aircraft again. The aircraft appears to have had an uneventful career, appearing at Gioia on May 16, 1945, where it passed its Preparation for Overseas Movement (POM) checks and returned to the US in June, where it was sent to Walnut Ridge, Arkansas, on November 30 for storage and eventual salvage.

Ferried from the US to the UK by a crew posted to 487th BG, this aircraft arrived on July 24, 1944. B-24J-DT 42-51284 was given 8th AF modifications and pooled (stored) at Base Air Depot (BAD) 3. The need for this aircraft as an immediate replacement was negated by the many former 3rd Bombardment Division B-24s as well as those from 489th BG, that had been taken off operations in November 1944, and were now available. It was released to 15th AF and transferred to Italy on December 12, 1944, where it was assigned to 722nd BS, 450th BG, on January 10, 1945, where it took up #44. Like the previous aircraft, it appeared at Gioia on May 16, from where it returned to the US for storage at Altus, Oklahoma.

This was a short-lived B-24. On October 14, 1944, B-24J-FO 42-51923 was assigned to 725th BS, 450th BG, and named *Short Stuff*. Less than a month later, on November 11, it was destroyed by fire on the ground.

Most officers in the air force were college-educated and many of them loved a pun or a double entendre in the names they painted on their aircraft. *Broad-Jumper* was B-24H-FO 42-52125 of 736th BS, 454th BG. On group mission #12, 30 aircraft from this group took off to bomb the Steyr-Daimler Pach aircraft factory, but due to bad weather the target was abandoned and alternates Graz and Klagenfurt airfields were hit. Between 40 and 50 Me-109s and FW-190s attacked the formation at Graz and eight B-24s were shot down, one of them being *Broad-Jumper* which, flown by Robert C. Forney, went into a spin and crashed. The missing air crew report for this aircraft is itself missing, so the fates of the individual crew members are not known.

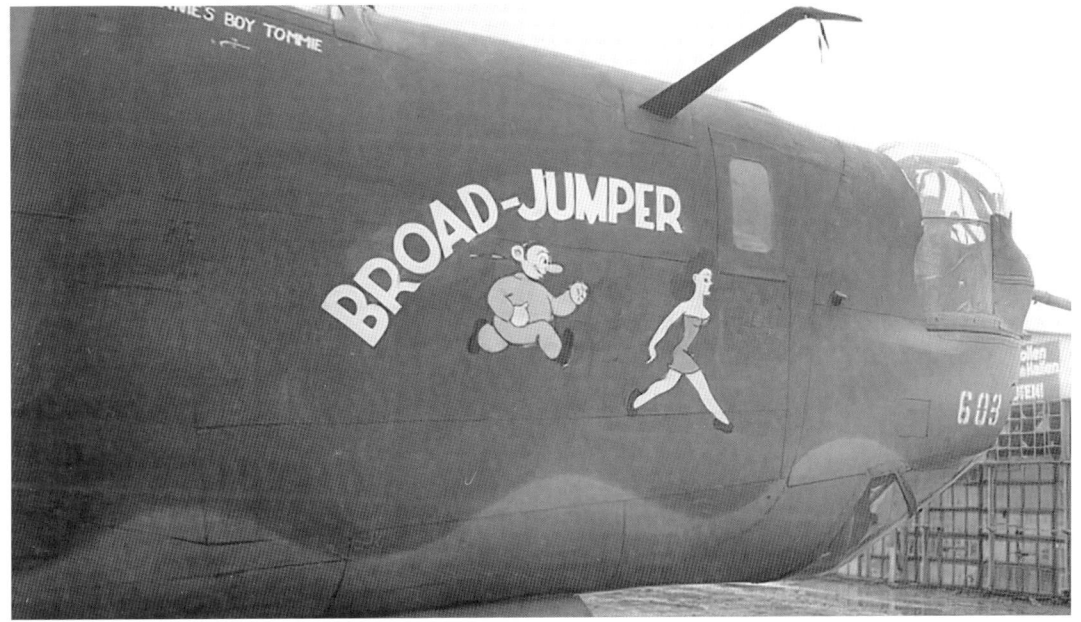

How low can you go? Not so low B-24J-DT 42-51332, #43, *Cherrie*, but the aircraft from which the photograph was taken! *Cherrie* joined the group on July 30, 1944, and served throughout the war. It returned to the US in June 1945, and by July 1 it had been ferried to Altus, Oklahoma, for open storage and eventual salvage.

Beautiful Takeoff was late model B-24L-FO 44-49732, which was not accepted by the USAAF until October 23, 1944. The aircraft record card does not show any overseas service, showing it reaching Greenville for storage in June 1945 until being sent to Kingman, Arizona, for further storage and salvage. 15th AF records, however, show it being allocated to 459th BG on March 31, 1945, giving at best a six-week combat history. The card is muddled somehow, because on this image the serial is legible. The destination code on the card indicates it is a one-off "special," and it spent eight weeks at the Convair modification centre at Nashville. 15th AF records have it sent to Gioia for return to the US, and the departure code later painted on the aircraft indicates a departure date of June 26.

Bea "R" Baby falls in a small serial range of Consolidated Fort Worth (-CF) B-24Hs. It was assigned to 747th BS, 456th BG as #66, 42-64470, and was damaged by flak over Friedrichshafen, Germany, on July 20, 1944, and opted to try and land in Switzerland rather than attempt the long trip home. Assessing the aircraft to be unsafe to attempt a crash landing, the crew abandoned the aircraft once over the Swiss border and were interned "for the duration."

This is some of the remains of *Bea "R" Baby* after it fell to earth after being abandoned by its crew.

The four B-24 wrecks, all B-24J-COs, are from the 461st BG, indicating that this is the 563rd Air Service Squadron "graveyard" at Torretta airfield, home base of the 461st. The nearest is almost certainly #71, 44-49584 of 767th BS, which crashed on January 31, 1945, and #18 is 44-41044 *Lady Duzz* of 764th BS, which crashed on take-off at Torretta on January 23, 1945. #11 is 42-51406 and suffered a similar fate on February 7, 1945. The most distant B-24, #23, is 44-41020 *Judy R* of 765BS, was salvaged on December 17, 1944. The B-17F *All American* is the famous 41-24406 of the 414th BS, whose tail was almost completely severed by an errant Bf-109 in February 1943. It was repaired, transferred to the 353rd BS and appears to have been used by the 461st as war-weary transport before salvage in March 1945. All have been stripped of usable parts before being taken to this location on the airfield.

It is difficult to determine what is happening here. B-24G 42-78383, B-Baker, of 760th BS, 460 BG, was written off on October 25, 1944, after running out of fuel and crash-landing two days previously. This photo does not appear to show any damage, but wherever it is, the aircraft isn't on a runway, taxiway or hardstand. The use of parachutes tied to the waist window machine gun pintles was the recommended way to slow an aircraft whose brakes had failed, although this looks more like a demonstration than a real situation.

Cruising above scattered cloud is B-24H-FO 42-95340, L-Love, named *Chick,* of 777 BS, 464 BG. On November 16, 1944, the aircraft was part of a mission to the Munich West rail marshalling yards. On the return journey, its low-fuel situation became critical, and calculations indicated that there was insufficient to return to base. The pilot, Lt. John W. Livermore, turned for Switzerland. During the landing approach, the aircraft stalled and crashed, but all members of the crew were uninjured. Though interned initially, the majority of the crew had been repatriated to the US by March 1945.

"Tin tappers" at Pantanella repair the 5,000th B-24 built by Consolidated at San Diego — specifically B-24J, L-Love, *V Grand 5000*, of 780th BS, 465th BG. As the 5,000th edition was a big deal, all those who worked for the company were permitted to sign the aircraft. The aircraft is known to have been forced to divert twice to the Croatian island of Vis on return from missions for engine changes each time. It returned to the US on June 8, 1945, and was sent to Altus, Oklahoma, for storage and salvage.

A stranger in a strange land — B-24G 42-78439 of 825th BS, 484th BG, at Dübendorf, Switzerland, wearing Swiss markings. On August 3, 1944, 2/Lt. Harry Schultz elected to take his aircraft to Switzerland when the oxygen system went out at 25,000ft well before the target and still with a full bomb load. He needed to descend to 10,000ft — alone and very vulnerable. Not named, at that time, it did however, carry nose art that represented a horned warrior holding a club in his left hand and grasping a lightning bolt in his right hand and the Squadron number 39. The Swiss removed all AAF and personal markings, adding their own, and flew this aircraft occasionally, but only with a close fighter escort. It was returned in June 1945 and arrived at Walnut Ridge for salvage on January 14, 1946.

Another B-24G but an earlier serial before the camouflage paint requirement was dropped. With *Sunsetter* art but no name, 42-78124, X-X-ray, was with 831st BS, 485th BG. 15th AF took control of the aircraft at the end of March 1944, and it flew combat until the end of the war. Most 15th AF aircraft that were capable of the journey were flown back to the US in June 1945, but it seems that '124 failed its POM inspection, was declared war weary and is recorded as salvaged at Gioia in August 1945.

A small formation of B-24s from the Desert Air Force overfly the airfield before descending and turning into the circuit for landing. An alert photographer has snapped them with the vertical stabilizer of a wrecked Ju-88 in the foreground, underlining the superiority of the Allied forces that now operate the previously German-controlled airfield.

The crew of B-24J-CO, 42-109854 *Cherry*, C-Charlie, from 415th BS are introduced to an officer-pilot of 98th BG while waiting to fly. *Cherry* flew missions from March 17, 1944, to October 10, before being declared war weary. It must have flown as a squadron hack for some time after that, as it was not salvaged until post-war.

B-24D 41-11613 carrying the third of three names it wore with a mission-expired crew on a Bond Tour throughout the US beginning in March 1944. Crew and aircraft went back to the USA and flew all over the country, displaying a hard-worked combat aircraft to crowds of people, gave speeches and people bought government bonds to help pay for the war. These bonds were repaid with interest at future dates. Originally *Florene Ju Ju*, HALPRO #10, in June 1942, it subsequently passed to 1 BG (P) (HALPRO SQN) and finally to 514th BS, 376th BG, #35, where it was renamed *Teggie Ann* after the daughter of 376th's Commanding Officer, Tegwin Ann. In December 1943, it became *The Blue Streak*, #71. As can be seen in the photo, the aircraft still looks well-worn despite a major rebuild to make it capable of the flight back to the US. On January 1, 1945, it was salvaged at Keesler AFB, the Mississippi headquarters of the 2nd AF.

B-24J-CF 44-10570, #43, of 717th BS, 449th BG, was struck by an 88mm flak shell, which did not explode until it reached the roof of the waist area, killing the two gunners and cutting the elevator and rudder cables. The pilot, Lt. Bernard L. Ball, brought the aircraft back from a Yugoslavian target to Bari on engines-only for pitch and yaw control. The exact date is not known, though August 1944 is usually quoted, making the aircraft almost brand new, it having only reached 15th AF on the 13th of the month. Not unexpectedly, the sight of this sort of destruction has drawn a large crowd, while the remaining NCOs and one officer, possibly the pilot, stand around shell-shocked trying to come to terms with what has happened to both the aircraft and their friends.

720th BS, 450th BG, PB-24J-FO 42-51554, #1, in standard 15th AF Pathfinder gray, drops a package of incendiaries over the target. The aircraft flew missions from October 12, 1944, and returned to the US on June 2, 1945. The SCR717C centimetric radar dome can be clearly seen protruding from the location of the ball turret on a standard-24 bomber.

On December 17, 1944, 451st BG on mission #168 was on its way to bomb the Odertal refinery in Poland when two 726th BS, B-24J-FOs came together. The #1 propeller of 42-52045, #55, cut the tail off 42-51941, #47, causing it to plummet vertically, with Lt. King and his crew trapped inside. The left wing of '045 was bent upward by the impact of the collision and tore #1 engine off. Several of the crew baled out shortly after the collision. After flying the stricken ship for several hours in an attempt to return to Italy, Lt. William Shelton and the remainder of his crew were able to bale out over Yugoslavia.

42-78377 *Easy Take*-Off, #61, was a long-lived combat B-24G. First assigned to the 738th BS, 454th BG, on June 5, 1944, it remained on strength to the end of the European war, accumulating 101 missions without any significant break outside of normal routine and major servicing and was still in sufficient condition to return to the US for salvage at Altus, Oklahoma, on October 1, 1945. Note the very different style of the North American factory anti-glare panel on the nose, a certain identifier of a B-24G.

Consolidated *Scrap Drive* began its combat career in 741st BS, 455th BG, #16, when the group was first formed, but was temporarily transferred to 343rd BS, 98th BG, during February and March 1944 when that group first arrived at Lecce from North Africa. It is known to have led the formation on the March 15, 1944 mission to Cassino, Italy, but turned back with the air speed indicator unserviceable. On March 20, 1944, it returned to 741st BS and its previous codes. On July 25, its crew baled out near San Severo because of damage to the aircraft. The photo shows that it lived up to its name.

April 12, 1944, was the end date for B-24H-FO 42-52292, #23, *Boojum* of 745th BS, 456th BG. On that day, *Boojum* was being flown by 2/Lt. Edward J. Meyer on group mission #29 to Bad Vöslau airfield, Austria. Just after releasing bombs on the target, the flight was attacked by more than 20 enemy fighters that made successive attacks and closed within 100 yards. Just a few minutes later, a large shell or rocket was observed to strike Lt. Meyer's aircraft and one engine was seen to be smoking badly. Almost immediately, one other engine was seen to flame and then one entire wing was ablaze. Lt. Meyer pulled up and away from the formation to the left and ten men were seen to parachute out. All parachutes opened and immediately the aircraft headed straight down toward the target, blazing all over.

For a 51-mission, shark-mouthed B-24H-FO with impressive art, little is known of *Cherokee Maiden*. A B-24H-FO 42-52427, it was received by 15th AF on January 19, 1944, and soon after allocated to 459th BG, which assigned it to 756th BS. It was one of the small number of B-24s to carry dual names, having *Chickie* inscribed on the right side of the nose. By December 1944, it had been reduced to war-weary status and salvaged at Gioia on April 17, 1945.

Nothing is known of this accident other than what can be deduced from the photo. The aircraft, 44-10549, T-Tare, a B-24J-CF (built by Consolidated but at its Fort Worth plant) belonged to 762nd BS, 460th BG. It looks like it may have had a tyre blow-out on take-off and subsequently left the runway and collapsed the right main undercarriage. The presence of the refuelling truck, in this case for de-fuelling the aircraft, suggests a take-off rather than a landing accident. It was written off on September 10, 1944.

How close can you get? It's a very tight and probably dangerous formation. This is another of the 8th AF replacements which, by the time they arrived, were no longer needed and so transferred to 15th AF. As shown by the markings, this B-24J-FO 42-51599, #34, is from the 765th BS, 461st BS, which is suggested to have been named *Peace Maker* or even *Piece Maker II*. The undersides are liberally splashed with mud, not unusual in Italy where runways were invariably created with pierced-steel planking (PSP) over bare earth and when it rained, it was muddy. '599 survived the war and returned to the US to be stored at Altus, Oklahoma, for later salvage.

Only minutes before, this plummeting streak of fire and smoke was a 464th BG B-24 manned by ten men. It remains unidentified as to serial or squadron or even date, but it is a reminder of the sacrifice made by airmen of the USAAF in the aerial conflict.

B-24H-FO 42-94747, #57, is a much-photographed aircraft of 856th BS, 484th BG. Initially just plain #57, it gained very sexy art created around the number and adapted from a Vargas calendar, then the shark mouth and finally the name *Dot's Right* were added. That name was later removed, and *Noveta Maria* added. It was retired from combat after 50 missions and became a war-weary transport with nose turret removed. It returned to the US on June 17, 1945.

Apart from the serial 42-78164, this anonymous-looking B-24G could be anywhere, but there are signs of its combat use. It would later pick up 15th AF yellow and black tail markings of the 485th BG and be flown with the 829th BS as U-Uncle. On July 30, 1944, it was shot down by flak after bombing the Duna aircraft factory in Budapest, Hungary. It fell in the Danube beside Csepel Island, Budapest South. Some parts of the aircraft, found close to the shore, have been recovered and are on display in the Szolnok Aviation Museum. Yellow strips on the bomb bay doors were a quick "tell" for other aircraft to know whether they were open or closed.

A much traveled lady. This pleasing image shows F-7 (the photographic reconnaissance version of the B-24D) 41-11673. Originally operated in the US in the 93rd BG's training phase before its departure to the 8th AF, it was one of three converted to the photo role at Bolling Field. It was named *Dragon Lady* after the Milton Caniff *Terry and the Pirates* comic strip. Assigned to the 1st Photo Mapping Squadron (PMS) of the 1st Photographic Group (PG) and coded Z-Zebra, it flew to North Africa in February 1943 in preparation for Operation *Torch*. On return to the US, it joined the 3rd PMS as a trainer at Kelly Field and was renamed *Ol' Nick*. *Dragon Lady was* moved to the other side of the nose. It continued its role when it moved to India with the 24th Combat Mapping Squadron (CMS), returning to the US in July 1944 but not salvaged until July 6, 1946.

B-24D 41-11766 *Chug-a-lug,* initially with 415th BS, 98th BG, B-Baker, flew missions from August 8, 1942, to March 3, 1943, before transfer to 345th BS as V-Victor where it flew further missions from March 24, 1943, to May 7, 1944. It flew on the infamous August 1, 1943, Ploești raid, and on the April 23, 1944, mission to Schwechat, Austria, was shot up, losing a turret and with the hydraulics put out. This ended its usefulness as a combat machine. It returned to the US on July 19, 1944, after 101 missions, and after plenty of publicity, it was retired. The write-off date is not known, as the aircraft card mistakenly has it shot down in Romania on August 10, 1943, but it is believed to have faded away in January 1946.

Shown here with one of 36 Lysander IIIs ordered by Turkey, is ex-HALPRO, #2, B-24D 41-11596, *Brooklyn Rambler*. It flew on the rushed first Ploești mission of June 12, 1942, but was interned in Turkey because of fuel shortage. The crew of Lt. Nathan Brown convinced the Turks that the aircraft needed to be flown occasionally. The Turks released a few gallons of fuel for that purpose and the crew flew practice missions, using slightly less fuel than the aircraft had on board. Turkish guards were always on board these practice missions. Slowly, the aircraft accumulated full tanks. On the day of the flight to Cyprus (January 1943) the crew convinced the guard to go get something. When he left the aircraft, the crew took off and navigated to Cyprus with a toy compass. At some later stage, the aircraft had a nosewheel collapse. The Turks were incensed at the "theft" of the aircraft and demanded it be returned. Instead, it was ferried to Gura (Eritrea) where Douglas Aircraft employees spent more than 8,000 hours repairing the aircraft, returning it to the Turks on March 27 at a cost to Uncle Sam of US$16,182.50 plus parts.

PB-24L-FO 44-49826, a 719th BS, 449th BG Pathfinder, displays an unusual field modification. This model B-24 is usually fitted with a lightweight turret and a pair of hand-held .50s, but this aircraft appears to sport a single, heavier calibre weapon. It joined the 719th on February 20, 1945, was ferried to Gioia on April 29 and landed back in the US on June 11. Its final fate was salvage at Walnut Ridge, Arkansas.

Seen crossing the Croatian coast and heading back to Italy across the Adriatic is B-24G 42-78154 of 722nd BS, 450th BG. On July 3, 1944, it was part of an attack on Giurgiu, Romania, flown by 1/Lt. Kenneth G. Wilson, and about two minutes short of the target the formation was hit with intense and accurate AA fire. '154 was struck in engine #3 and the associated fuel tanks burst into flames. As the aircraft left the formation, six men baled out in quick succession, followed by a further three and the last after a short pause. All ten parachutes were reported to have been seen to open, however post-war reports indicate that the bombardier was burned in the aircraft and jumped with his 'chute on fire, the engineer jumped without a 'chute in panic, and the top turret gunner was shot on the ground.

#33, the nearest of the aircraft, B-24J-FO 42-51999 of 725th BS, has crossed the Alps into Austria as part of the high element of 451st BG formation; note the low element far below. On March 20, 1944, the aircraft flew as #999 because the 451st was changing its numbering system that day — not for the first time either, to the confusion of historians later — returning as #36 on its next mission. A lucky aircraft, it flew to the end of hostilities, returned to the US and was salvaged at Walnut Ridge, Arkansas.

Just why B-24J-CO 44-41142 (coded R-Roger) was trying to land in Poltava, Ukraine, on January 4, 1945, remains unknown. No missing air crew report was raised, so its "arrival" must have been advised to 780th BS, 465th BG within 24 hours. The accident occurred in dense fog and I imagine that there were no alternate fields available; it was land or bale out. The pilot was Ralph E. Beam and from the presence of the recovery vehicle, US forces could not have been too far away.

This was not the only B-24 known to be named *Gentleman Jim*; a 43rd BG B-24 in the Pacific was also so named, both no doubt named after heavyweight boxing champion James J. Corbett. This particular *Gentleman Jim* was 42-52263, #32, operating with 737th BS, 454th BG. It flew missions regularly up to January 20, 1945, when it suffered a Category 3 landing accident at the hands of Russel J. Frick, which caused the aircraft to be sent to Gioia Depot for repair. It returned to the squadron for a month on April 17 only to be returned to Gioia on May 16, never to return, being downgraded to war-weary status and salvaged in June. If you look closely, you will see that whoever Jim was punching has been erased.

743rd BS, 455th BG, B-24H-CF 42-64500 appears to being checked; its nosewheel has jammed in the down position. There are no accident reports for the aircraft so it must have all ended happily. Not such a happy day for *Dazzlin' Dutchess and the Ten Dukes* was the June 11, 1944-attack on Giurgio, Romania, with 2/Lt. Earl W. Braminger as command pilot. Prior to reaching the target, the aircraft was observed to make a 180-degree turn back towards Italy. No reason for this could be seen, but it was thought likely to be because of previously reported fuel leaks. A burning aircraft was observed in Bulgaria by the formation during its return from the target, but it could not be identified. Post-war enquiries revealed that the crew had baled out over Romania, but one had drowned in the Danube. Another was unfortunately killed by a German dive-bomber attack just after Romania had been liberated.

Not marked the way you would expect, B-24J-CO 44-41108, *Duchess,* of 747th BS, 456th BG, was found by US troops on April 24, 1945, at Cham between Regen and Schwarzenfeld, a large and active base. It was reported lost on March 25, 1945, in Russia, but because of mechanical failure it had been forced to land by German fighters at Piestany Airfield (in Slovakia, not Russia as mentioned) and consequently used by 2/KG200 in German markings. The nine crew were made POW for a short period.

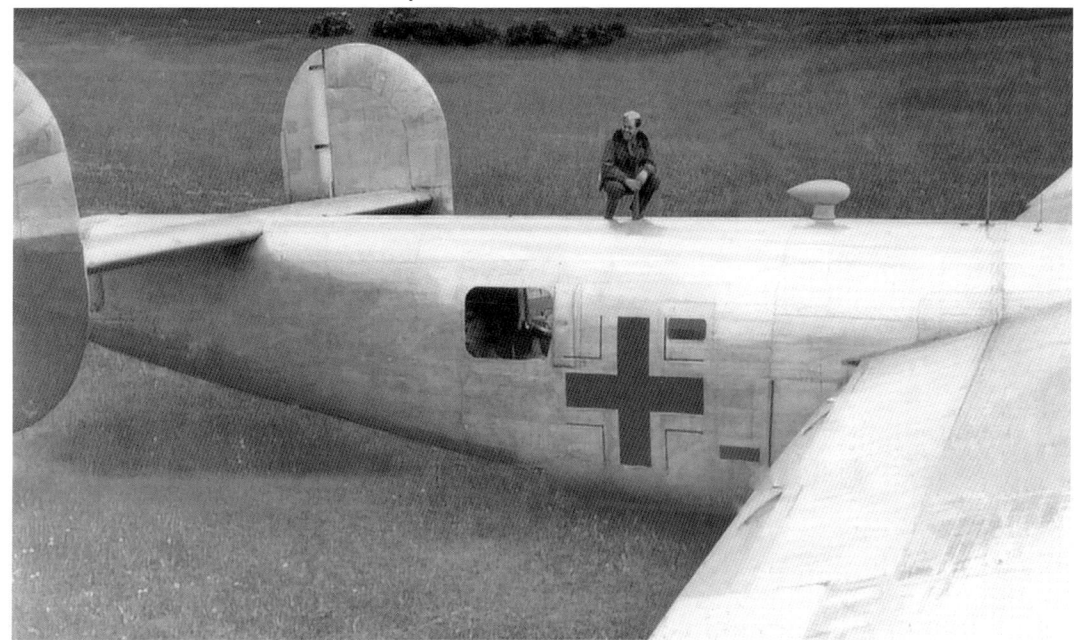

A pair of B-24s from 459th BG. The distant aircraft is 44-10565 (7E) (see page 58) and PB-24 44-49532 *The Cryin' Lion* of 757th BS in Pathfinder gray, coded #7O. It had been received by the unit on December 26, 1944, and served to the end of hostilities. At Gioia, after the war, its return code was noted to indicate a planned return date to the US of June 26, 1945, and it was parked and shut down for the last time at Kingman, Arizona, for storage and salvage on December 9, 1945.

Stripped of all useful parts, four 15th AF B-24s lie in the graveyard at Gioia. Only one is identifiable, the 484th BG aircraft in the foreground whose serial can be read as 42-94739, from 826th BS, #60, and named *Sleepy Time Gal*, which was declared war-weary in February 1945 and salvaged in March. *Bottoms up!* another B-24H-FO and from 460th BG, coded C-Charlie (identified by the group black panther on the nose), lies behind. The name was very common among B-24s and has not yet been attached to a specific serial and therefore its squadron also remains unknown.

Crossing the threshold — attitude good, speed good, descent rate on the numbers, touch down imminent: how to land a B-24! B-24J-FO 42-51759, #47, of 766th BS, 461st BG, on short-short final for the runway at Torretta. Apart from a diversion to the Croatian island of Vis for mechanical assistance on the return from a mission on March 15, 1945, it appears to have been a reliable bird to fly. It departed Gioia for the US post-war and arrived on July 26, 1945, ending its days at Altus, Oklahoma.

B-24H-FO 42-95332 *The Flak Man*, U-Uncle, of 779th BS, 464th BG, on its PSP hardstand at Pantanella displaying seven Swastikas as claims for fighters shot down — a doubtful tally but good for morale. '332 was involved in three relatively minor accidents in 1945: the first was a taxi accident at Falconara on January 20, and the second a landing accident at Pantanella on March 19. It returned to service on April 12, just before the end of the war. It returned to the US and was taken over by the government agency the Reconstruction Finance Company at Walnut Ridge, Arkansas, in October 1945.

When we climb the serial ranges into the 44–49 range (B-24L-FO) and beyond, it means these aircraft were delivered to their combat units in 1945, thus limiting their combat careers to five months or less. The location of this image, over the Alps, is not a place where you would want to bale out. This is PB-24 44-49763, N-Nan, which had an even shorter career, having been delivered to 783rd BS, 465th BG, on February 20, 1945, and crashing on landing on March 29 at Pantanella and being written off.

The 484th BG lost one of its more outrageously nicknamed aircraft when B-24G 42-78351, #34, *Aaah! What's Up Doc?* crashed — not so much the name because cartoon-related names were quite popular — but because of the extravagant manner in which it was painted. This 825th BS aircraft was originally named *The Rover Boys* in the US by its ferry crew, but when it arrived in the squadron, M/Sgt Harold C. Jacobs changed it. On December 10, 1944, the #2 engine caught fire at about 50ft on take-off. While still climbing but returning to the field, at 300ft the remaining three engines quit and the crew crash-landed with a full load of booby-trap 500-pounders and fuel. All 11 aboard survived uninjured, except for the navigator who cut his foot when the nose wheel strut broke.

Above: *Flak Shak II*, most likely B-24J-CO 44-40444, G-George, of 831st BS, 485th BG, which was lost on the Munich attack on July 19, 1944, while being flown by Capt. John C. Sandall and his 829th BS crew. Over the target, the #2 engine was hit by flak, which tore off the left wing. Only three parachutes were seen and they belonged to a gunner, the engineer and bombardier, who became POWs. The remainder were killed in action.

Right: One of 159 Squadron's Liberator IIs being "bombed up" with 1,000-pounders at Fayid in North Africa prior to a mission.

B-24 Liberator: Combat Photographs from the Mediterranean Theater of War

B-24D 42-40322 *The Cornhusker*, K-King, just airborne at Benina, Libya, and the base for 415th BS, 98th BG. *Cornhusker* flew missions from April 28, 1943, until the August 1, 1943-low-level Ploești mission. The 98th were in tight formation on the return from Ploești over the Ionian Sea when crewmen in other aircraft noticed the #2 propeller was feathered, and the #4 engine, which had lost a massive amount of oil, caught fire. It is not known how the damage happened, but it is assumed that it was caused by ground fire over the target. The aircraft dropped back and lost height rapidly. After several thousand feet were lost, six men were observed to bale out; four 'chutes opened and two men were seen hitting the water. The aircraft struck the water and exploded. None aboard were recovered. The original caption to the photo claimed it was landing, but the flap setting suggests otherwise.

Pre-dawn, August 1, 1943, Benghazi, Libya. Aircrew of the 376th BG disembark from their transport. Some prepare to board their aircraft, *Teggie Ann,* #100, (see page 6). The rest, on the truck, will shortly be taken to their aircraft. For some, no doubt, this was their last day on earth as this was the start of Operation *Tidal Wave*, the statistics for which are spelled out in the introduction to this book.

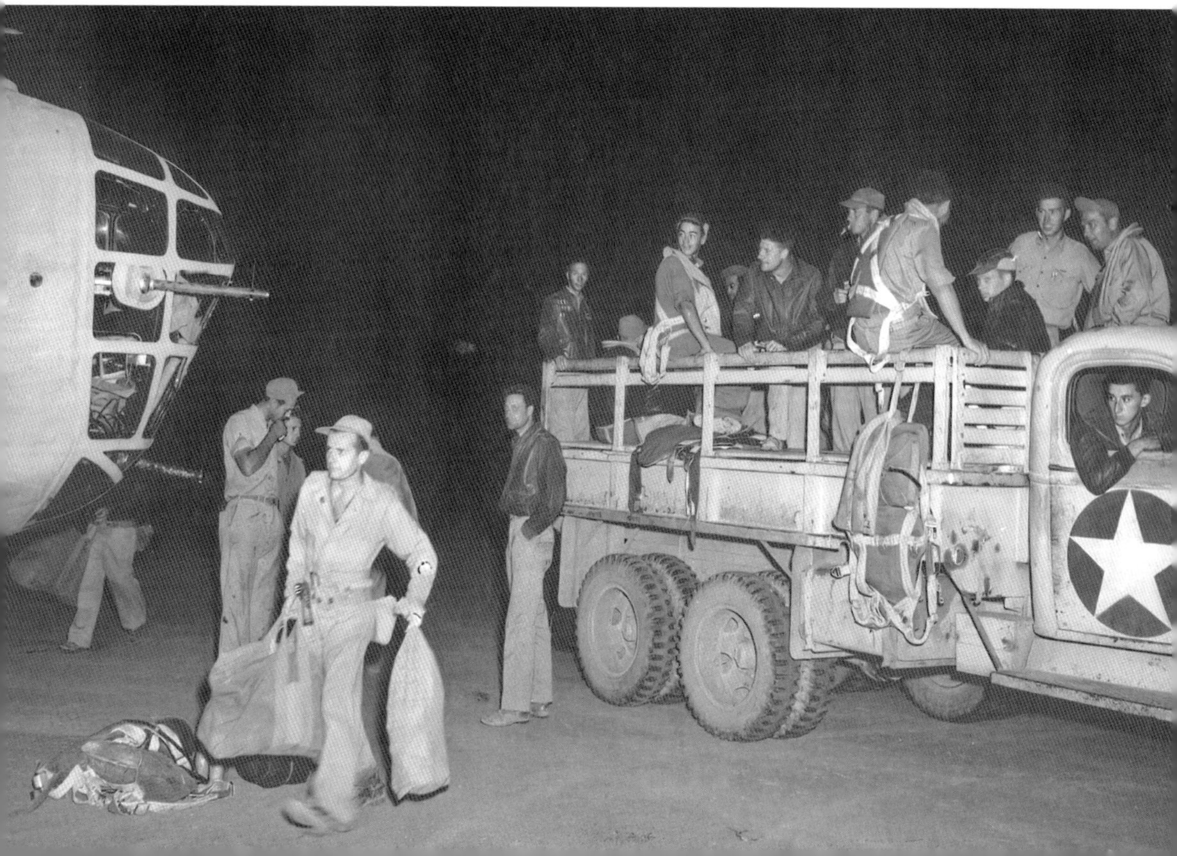

Originally #51 but later #66, B-24H-FO 42-52140, *Ghost O' The Omar*, was assigned to 716th BS, 449th BG, while working up in Bruning, Nebraska, in the US. The original Browning crew named it in memory of the cocktail lounge of the Continental Hotel, Kansas City, Missouri, which was popular before overseas deployment. Flown by 2/Lt James P. Collins on the June 9, 1944, Porto Marghera mission, it was damaged by flak over Udine, Italy, when the formation was still on the way to the target. Unable to keep up and already north of the Alps, it was turned and headed back towards base but was abandoned by the crew approaching Salzburg. The aircraft crashed near Klagenfurt and the crew was captured.

This is the sort of damage an 88mm German flak shell can cause. On the 450th BG's 81st mission to the Castel Maggiori rail marshalling yards on June 5, 1944, 722nd BS, B-24G 42-78334, #44, suffered this damage, but the aircraft managed to return safely. The fact that it was repaired in time to take part in the June 26 mission to the Schwechat aircraft factory in Austria suggests that an outer wing section was salvaged from the graveyard for the repair. However, it was on this mission that '334 was shot down, being hit in #4 engine, which caught fire over the target. All crew baled out and were captured in Hungary.

Another take-off photograph. This time it is B-24G 42-78463, #61, of 727th BS, 450th BG, at Castelluccio. It was listed as missing in action (MIA) on mission #187 to Vienna on February 7, 1945, and a missing air crew report was raised. After the aircraft sustained battle damage, 1/Lt. Glenn A. Kerres called for a course to Vis and the crew stayed with the aircraft until it ran out of fuel. They baled out, and the aircraft crashed near Pettrovic, Croatia. All were returned to duty with the help of Partisans.

Most photos of this aircraft are of the art and omit the name! *Good Heavens* was B-24J-CO 44-41059 of 736th BS, 454th BG. It was the artillerymen of Villach, Austria, who sent the aircraft and some of its crew to their own heaven when it joined the November 11, 1944 attack on the rail marshalling yards. Their accuracy put a shell into the nose of the aircraft, killing all forward of the bomb bay and made the remainder POWs after they baled out at low level.

On December 16, 1944, B-24G 42-78360, #48, of 742nd BS, 455th BG, was departing San Giovanni Field, Italy, as part of a group bombing mission to Brüx, Germany. From the accident report: "Aircraft mushed on take-off and bounced, breaking off left main landing gear. Upon instructions from Wing Commander, plane was flown until gasoline supply was exhausted. Pilot decided to have seven crew members bale out and then brought the aircraft to Gioia A.F." Not mentioned is the rather obvious requirement that if you are going to crash-land you need to dispose of the bomb load first. Picking up the aircraft, *Fubar II*, is the AAF's equivalent of the Navy's Tillie, able to lift the complete aircraft and move it away from the runways and taxiways. In polite parlance, FUBAR is "Fouled Up Beyond All Recognition."

Generally known as the *Gallopin' Galoot*, 745th BS, 456th BG, B-24H-DT 41-28810, #39, is also quoted as a Pathfinder, but here can be seen a ball turret where the radar dome should be. It appears that this aircraft was converted in the field, after service without radar. During an undated mission, Lt. Robert Engelbert and crew landed at the Croatian island of Vis after a hectic return flight from the target. They had a severely damaged tail assembly, one rudder was inoperative and actually fluttering as they flew. Thought had been given to baling out over Yugoslavia but they managed to nurse the ship to Vis where a successful landing was made. On another occasion, it ran out of brakes and collided with 42-78623, but its final fate was a crash on December 5, 1944.

With #3 engine throwing a little oil, B-24J-CF 44-10626 (7E) crosses the Alps into Austria, its 459th BG black-and-yellow-checked tail prominent. The 7E code determines that it was assigned to 757th BS. There is no significant information associated with this aircraft other than it did not return to the US, being salvaged at Gioia on July 30, 1945. Often claimed to be named either *Ginny* or *Ginnie*, no photographic evidence of this has yet surfaced.

A formation of 460th BG B-24s over Salzburg. These fires are not caused by bombing and may have been lit to obscure the areas likely to be targeted; a pall of smoke haze has built up downwind of the fires.

B-24H-FO 42-95304, #42, of 766th BS, 461st BG being prepared for a mission, bombs loaded. On December 17, 1944, this aircraft was attacked by fighters just short of the Oferta 1 refinery target in Germany and one engine was damaged. The pilots tried to feather the propeller but it would not comply and the windmilling prop shook the aircraft badly. It was last seen south of Bratislava, Czechoslovakia, maintaining height but lower than the formation. The aircraft was later known to have crashed near Karlovac, Croatia, and as the crew was captured, it is assumed that it eventually had to abandon the aircraft.

Two of these three aircraft of the 464th BG are in trouble. One, O-Oboe, has a smoking #2 engine, which may have developed into something much worse, and the other is already going down. Close examination of the photo suggests that the crew have already begun to bale out. Since the image is not dated, it is not possible to definitively put an identity to any of them, though L-Love is most likely 42-95340 *Chick* of 777th BS, indicating that the other two aircraft are also from 777th BS.

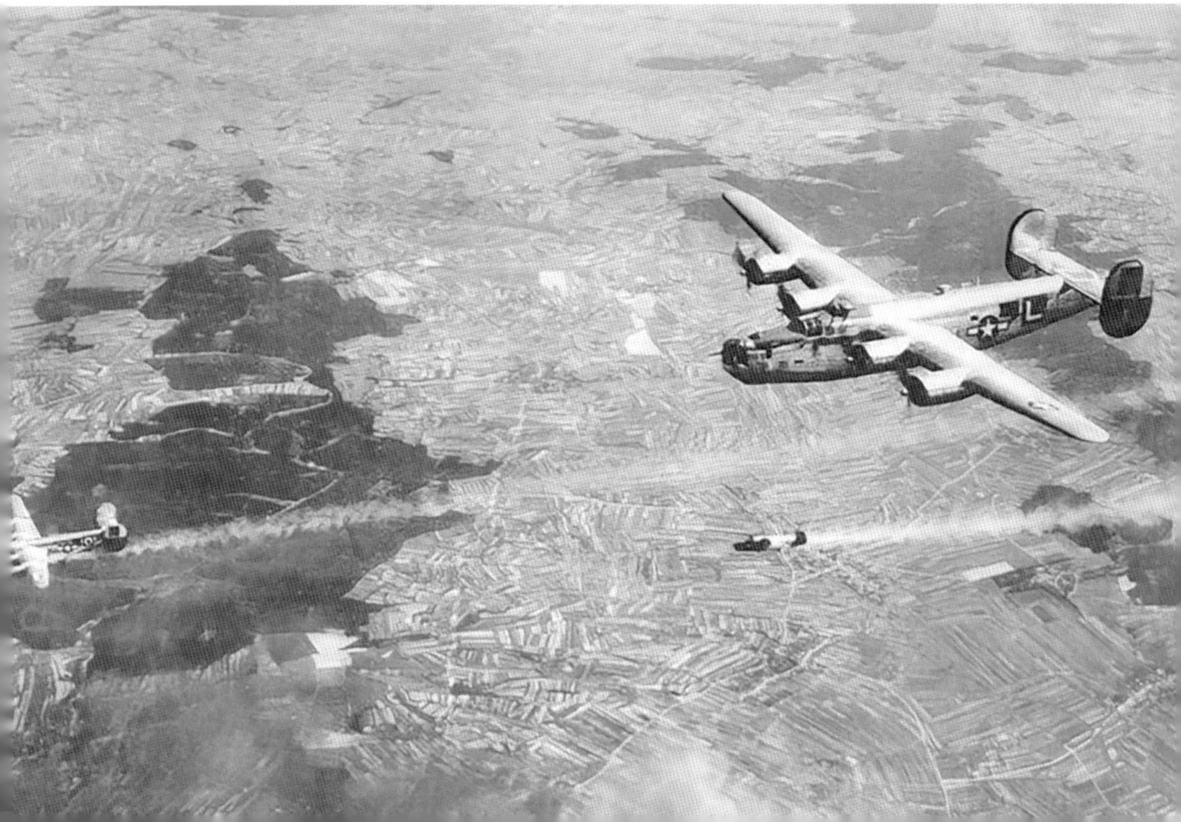

Another B-24 in major trouble, this time from 465th BG; once a fire starts in an inboard fuel tank, the aircraft is doomed. This is 41-29356 *Cluster's Folly*, G-George, of 781st BS. Hit by fighters and flak on May 30, 1944, on the Wiener Neustadt mission, it was seen to fall into a spin over Yugoslavia and at 4,000ft it exploded, throwing out three of the crew who had not by then baled out and killing the pilot and navigator. The eight survivors were aided by partisans and successfully reached Allied lines.

A happy looking crew pose beside B-24H-FO 42-52730, X-X-ray, *Big Alice From Dallas*, of 829th BS, 485th BG, after completing its 50th mission. Noting a liquor bottle front and centre, it seems they may have toasted the aircraft with a tot. There is one too many men for a full crew in the photo, the 11th man is the crew chief at the far left. *Big Alice* ended its flying career on October 10, 1944, when it crash-landed at Venosa with the hydraulics shot out.

A flight of 485th BG B-24s crosses the south-western tip of Vis after leaving the main European coast on a heading that appears to be direct to Bari. The lower of the two camouflaged aircraft, coded H-How, is 42-52724 *Buzz Job*. Vis was a last chance diversion point, not occupied by Axis troops, and with an emergency runway cut into a grape vine crop. Repair facilities were available and fuel for those who were running short. Between there and the AAF bases in southern Italy, there was nothing but the Adriatic Sea. The sea floor around Vis is littered with Allied aircraft that tried and did not make it, mainly B-24s and B-17s — an attraction today for divers.

Late afternoon and a B-24H from the 15th AF has just crossed the landing threshold of one of the Foggia-complex of bomber airfields in southern Italy, no doubt at the end of a long mission into the "soft underbelly of Europe." Off to the left is another B-24, its left main undercarriage leg broken, the victim of an earlier emergency landing.

The third of the 343rd BS B-24s to have been named *Dopey* is B-24D 42-41014. A few more followed; I know of at least six, all with the 343rd BS. This one had an additional feature, being named *Jolly Roger* on the other side. This wreck was the result of a take-off accident at Lecce on April 17, 1944. Its first mission with the 98th BG was on September 3, 1943. Number 4, B-24J-CF 42-64393 *Dopey*, flew its first mission one week after this accident.

B-24D 41-11620 *Edna Elizabeth*, was an original HALPRO aircraft, #16, and followed the other survivors through 1st BG (P) (HALPRO Squadron), which became 513th BS, 376th BG. It suffered a nosewheel collapse in March 1943, after which its name was changed (in chalk) to *The Flying Shim* and the number to 15 7/8ths! It was sent to Project 19 Base, Eritrea, where it was fully repaired, as per this photograph, and on return went to 343rd BS, 98th BG, Z Zebra, but still named *Edna Elizabeth*. It was on the August 1, 1943 Ploești mission but aborted, and because it continued to be a rogue ship mechanically, it was removed from combat after September 22, 1943. What it did after that is anybody's guess, probably sitting in various depots unserviceable, as it was not slated for return to the US until May 1944. The ferry took four months, after which it was deemed Class 26 and relegated to an instructional airframe. Beyond that, it just faded away, there not being a specific end date recorded.

An apparently happy crew pose beside *Maw Stricknine* showing 35 missions. I say apparently, because if you look at their eyes you will see the strain and weariness of those missions. This was B-24H-FO 42-52104 of 716th BS, 449th BG, variously #49, #64 and #66, as it came and went to depots for maintenance and repair. An original group aircraft, it was sent for major overhaul in mid-1944. On completion, it was sent to 98th BG and assigned to 345th BS only as a hack, it would appear, as it shows in no mission records. Returned to Gioia in December 1944, it was salvaged there on August 15, 1945, after accident damage.

On February 25 1945, B-24J-CO 44-41188, #35, of 721st BS, 450th BG, was at 24,000ft over the rail marshalling yards at Linz, Austria, bomb door open and only seconds from the drop when an 88mm flak shell struck the nose, smashing the nose turret and blowing off most of the skin of the aircraft forward of the cockpit. The aircraft initially went out of control and almost struck another in the formation, then rolled left and dropped away, all engines functioning and under control. Without further sighting reports from aircrew, it can only be surmised that bale out orders were given immediately and the crew still alive exited the aircraft quickly. How the pilots survived is a miracle. The navigator, bombardier and nose gunner were killed instantly and the remainder were captured.

B-24J-CF 44-10613 is seen here crossing the Alps. It was originally assigned to 726th BS, 451st BG, as #44, on August 20, 1944, and appears to have flown with that unit until December when it transferred to a maintenance depot. The documentation changing its unit to 461st BG is absent; all that is known is that it was with 461st at some point prior to returning to the US in May 1945, but it could be that it was flown back by a 461st crew.

Very nicely framed by an non-airworthy B-24 are a pair of 454th BG aircraft undergoing maintenance. *Hairless Joe*, B-24H-FO 42-52228, arrived in Italy on January 12, 1944, and was assigned to 738th BS as #77. On July 20, 1944, it was taking part in an attack on Friedrichshafen flown by 1/Lt. Charles H. Hilton. Over the target at 20,000ft, it was hit by flak between #3 and #4 engines and immediately flamed before the wing broke off at #3 engine. The aircraft went out of control and, after diving for thousands of feet, entered a flat spin. Only one man managed to exit the aircraft to be captured, the rest dying on board.

Apart from this accident, this particular B-24 had one unusual claim to fame: built with a hydraulic Consolidated nose turret, it was one of few that was field-converted — one assumes because of damage to the original — with an electric Emerson turret. Assigned to 740th BS, 455th BG, as #15, it was serialled as B-24J-CF 42-64234 and named *Ghost of a Chance*. It finished up in this ditch after running out of fuel (and no doubt hydraulics and brakes) and making an emergency landing at Gioia.

I am not sure of the significance of *Gin Rae*, but there is a bottle of gin in the illustration and I guess the female must be Rae. This is B-24J-CO 42-109839, #53, of 746th BS, 456th BG, assigned on March 24, 1944. The 456th initially used numbers to identify their aircraft, but between the missions of December 6 and 9, 1944, these were replaced by individual letters, in a squadron color, placed on the rear fuselage aft of the waist gun windows; *Gin Rae*'s code #53 became N-Nan. In March 1945, it went to Gioia for a major overhaul and never returned.

Looking at the limited snow coverage on the ranges below, this is a summer 1944 photograph; the aircraft was delivered to the 459th BG in late January 1944. It is B-24H-FO 42-52356 named *Hot Sketch*. 2/Lt. Glenn C. Raiter, Jr. and his 756th BS crew took *Hot Sketch* on the August 25, 1944-mission to Kúria, Czechoslovakia, and were heading home when it was noticed that the aircraft was dropping back with one propeller feathered and the others not developing full power. One P-51 of the 325th Fighter Group (also adorned with yellow-and-black tails like the 459th) escorted the aircraft to Yugoslavia. Raiter asked the fighter pilot to count nine crew baling out and to advise him so that he could then bale out. They were down to 11,000ft by this time. The pilot later reported seeing ten 'chutes. All subsequently returned to the squadron by September with the help of Partisans, although some had injuries from the rough country into which they had parachuted.

B-24G 42-78260 named *Gal 'O Mine II*, oddly punctuated, flew with the 763rd BS, 460th BG. This photograph must have been taken close to the aircraft's arrival with the squadron (May 1944), as it is not yet marked with Group tail insignia or squadron code. The smoke from the fire below could only have come from an oil refinery. The 460th flew three missions to various parts of the Ploești refinery complex, Romania, in May 1944. '260 barely had time to be painted as #71, before it was shot down over Giurgiu by flak on June 11. Only eight parachutes were noted, but subsequently all members of the crew were found to have survived.

On D-Day, June 6, 1944, 1/Lt. John F. Ware and crew were part of yet another bombing mission on the Ploești oilfield complex as part of the 778th BS, 464th BG, B-24H-DT 41-28755 *Hard Hearted Hannah*. A few minutes after the bombs were dropped, observers in other aircraft noticed that '755 seemed to be experiencing some difficulty keeping up with the formation and maintaining height. Shortly after, "three or four" men were seen to exit the aircraft. At this point, fighters attacked the formation and when the battle was over, there was no sign of '755 and it never reappeared. The MACR for the aircraft (which has disappeared) showed that "all but three crew returned to duty." Other information states that the aircraft landed on a barricaded runway at Sidi Sarigazi Field, approximately 15 miles northeast of Istanbul, Turkey, and that the aircraft was written off. The fate of the three who baled out is not known.

This is one lucky crew. On March 9, 1945, B-24H-FO 42-95344, #70, of 767th BS, 461st BG, was over Austria at 29,000ft and had just dropped its bombs on the rail marshalling yards at Graz when the bombardier advised that there was "no flak here," so the pilot began a descent to speed the exit from the target area. Just then, a 105mm flak shell entered the aircraft through the open bomb bay and exploded against the roof of the radio position, destroying it. The radioman was in the waist area about to head to his station and send the "bombs away" message and escaped injury, not to mention death! Most of the blast shot back through the open bomb bay, cutting the rudder control cables, knocking out the interphone and oxygen systems and causing a fuel leak. The pilots flew the aircraft back to Cerignola and landed without brakes, rolling off the end of the runway. The man in the shell hole is tail gunner S/Sgt. Raymond B. Spencer, who was on his 31st mission. The aircraft was repaired but was lost in a crash-landing on May 30, 1945.

Just exactly what all these people are doing at the end of the runway is unknown — engineers considering lengthening it maybe — but the location is undeniable. This is the emergency runway on the Isle of Vis. The aircraft is B-24H-DT 41-28917, C-Charlie, of 782nd BS, 465th BG, named *Ferp Finesco*, which crash-landed in October 1944 at Vis with #1 engine shut down. The unusual name was created by taking the first letter of each crewman's home town name, and fashioning it into something that could be pronounced. Post-war it made it back to the US for salvage at Altus, Oklahoma.

B-24H-FO 42-52633 *Darling Darlene* arrived in the Mediterranean Theatre of Operations on April 14, 1944. Documentation showing its assignment is missing until February 1945 when it appears with 826th BS, 484th BG, though it probably flew with 484th BG from May 1944. It returned to the US at the end of May 1945 for salvage at Albuquerque, New Mexico.

This is part of the wreckage of B-24H-CF 42-50414, *Gawgia Peach*, B-Baker, of 831st BS, 485th BG, which replaced a previous *Gawgia Peach*, lost on June 13, 1944. From the diary of Hank Dahlberg, 831st engineering officer, 47-mission pilot, Lt. Young B. (Ben) Barber was slow-timing the engines and took two mechanics, two refuelling specialists and an aircraft guard from the base guard along for the ride. He did not have a co-pilot, but had his navigator or bombardier flying in the co-pilot's seat. Barber was shutting down various engines when he crashed not far from base. The others survived, but Barber was not wearing his seatbelt. He fractured his skull and died while being taken to hospital. He had only three more missions to fly to finish his tour.

From the inscription on the bottom of this image it has a Turkish origin. *Gump the Sniffer* was B-24D 41-23763, X-X-ray, of 345th BS, 98th BG, no doubt posted in from 1 BG (P), which is where the early radar-equipped (SCR-521) aircraft were billeted in the interim period in North Africa. "Sniffer" was the code for radar at the time. Captain Thomas T. Omohundro and a scratch crew set out at 20 30hrs on February 15, 1943, on a reconnaissance mission from LG159 (RAF Base Gambut 5) over Italy. They experienced major difficulties with icing, #3 engine catching alight and various turbocharger failures, but a 150mph tail-wind took them way off course and with only 15 minutes of fuel remaining, Omohundro selected the largest field available and landed after 12 hours in the air, the nosewheel hitting a ditch, which also took out the left main undercarriage. The Turks interned and dismantled the aircraft.

On August 22, 1944, Lt. Charles Andrews was flying B-24J-CO 44-40330, #92, *Hardway Ten*, a craps term, "ten the hard way," and was badly shot up on a mission around Vienna, losing both engines on the left side, brakes, hydraulic power, as well as oxygen, among other things. He was determined to get it back to base, but it was difficult to fly in a straight line and had to be flown with the right wing raised quite a bit and it did not hold height. With a likely chance of ditching in the Adriatic, the decision was made to attempt a landing at Vis. When Andrews turned in to land he was committed, unable to go around or turn back. A B-24 with a blown tire was on the runway, shortening the landing run; then an Italian transport plane pulled out on the runway without bothering to look and see if anyone was coming. At that moment, Andrews knew that he would have to crash and the left gear hit an irrigation ditch, and threw the aircraft on its back. Three were killed.

When you reach late-serial B-24M-FOs like this one, 44-50496, their delivery dates made their combat time extremely short, exacerbated in this case by it having been originally an 8th AF replacement, which was surplus to requirements. After some storage time, it was released to the 15th AF and assigned to 720th BS, 450th BG, on March 8, 1945. The 450th flew its last mission on April 26, allowing a possible maximum seven weeks of mission opportunities. On May 16, it flew to Gioia and by July 1 it was back in the US and the Reconstruction Finance Company stored it at Walnut Ridge.

Holy Joe was not a long-lived aircraft. B-24H-CF 41-29224, #45, and later #36, was original equipment of 717th BS, 449th BG, flown by Lt. Fowler's crew to Italy between December 7 and 26, 1943. The 449th BG flew its first combat mission on January 8, 1944. The first photograph shows the aircraft at Rufisque, Dakar, during the ferry flight, a few days before Christmas Day 1943. The crew would not have hung around Rufisque: it was hot and dusty, the accommodation poor and the food terrible. No doubt they would have aimed to have been in a more salubrious location to celebrate Christmas. On March 29, 1944, just as the aircraft broke ground at Bruning on take-off, fully loaded for a mission, one engine failed. Lt. Ivers had no option but to try and crash-land. Two of the crew were killed and the other eight were all injured, two seriously enough to be permanently grounded and the others returned to duty. Lt. Fowler quickly named the replacement aircraft (42-5028) as *Holy Joe II*, which arrived on April 1, but it lasted only a fortnight, being shot down on the Brasov mission, Romania.

Two 726th BS, 451st BG, B-24s are seen here, still climbing to assigned altitude as they cross the Alps, northbound. The nearer aircraft, 42-51677, #50, *Skylark* is a B-24J-FO, which returned to the US on May 18, 1945, for storage at Kingman, Arizona. The other, which carries art of a female, is not named and is B-24J-CF 44-10630, #46, which crashed and was written off on November 11, 1944.

Miss Maggie was B-24H-FO 42-52207, #63, of 738th BS, 454th BG, photographed here with a ground staff member after completing its 50th mission. Flown to Italy between December 11 and 31, 1943, by Lt Hugh N. West, Jr. and crew, by November 20, 1944, it had been downgraded to war-weary status. It appears to have remained with the 454th as a transport, returning to the US on March 23, 1945, for storage at Altus, Oklahoma.

An oft-repeated strategy of AAF photographers was to have someone pretend to be just completing a piece of art on an aircraft for a photograph, as is the case here. *"Glammer Gal"*, B-24H-FO 42-52198, was original equipment of 742nd BS, arriving in Italy with 455th BG in January 1944. During take-off for the December 16, 1944, mission to Brux, Germany, the aircraft mushed and bounced, breaking off the left landing wheel. Upon instructions from the Wing Commander, the aircraft was flown until the fuel supply was exhausted, the pilot electing to have seven crew members bale out before bringing the aircraft to Gioia for the landing. After repair, it was declared war-weary and sent to 449th BG as a hack, where it was renamed as *Turd Bird*! It was salvaged at Gioia in August 1945.

Not so lucky early model B-24G (fifth last to receive factory paint when the requirement was dropped) 42-78183, *Lucky 'leven*, #35, of 745th BS, 456th BG. Taken on charge by 15th AF on March 26, 1944, and subsequently assigned to 456th BG, it was parked at its 745th BS hardstand at Stornara on June 11 when an RAF Halifax, probably from No.148 (Special Duties) Squadron, lost control during the take-off and collided with it.

The original caption to this photo says: "April 12, 1945. American and Russian personnel wave their greetings as the Consolidated B-24 *Judith Ann* carrying Major General [William] Deane [C.G. 44th Infantry Division] and Major General Edmund W. Hill [C.G. USAAF in Russia], comes to a halt on the steel mat runway at Poltova Airbase, a shuttle mission base in Russia." The aircraft is B-24L-FO 44-49771, #6E, of 756th BS, 459th BG. Less than two weeks later, on 25 April, the aircraft was shot down on what must have been the Group's last World War Two mission, to Linz, Austria. The pilot stated that he had been hit and would try for Russia, but the damage must have been greater than was initially thought as the crew baled out in Southern Austria.

B-24G 42-78419 *Helen*, F-Fox, of 760th BS, 460th BG, over the foothills, begins the climb to cross the Alps in what looks like high summer 1944. On August 29, it was lost on a mission to Ostrava, Czechoslovakia. After leaving the target, the aircraft was observed to leave the formation on a heading, suggesting it was intending to land at Vis possibly short of fuel, due to flak damage. Two P-38s saw the lone aircraft and escorted it, but it made a crash-landing from which some of the crew were seen to exit, but the location was "lost in translation." The fact that all crew members were returned to the US in November 1944 suggests that it was probably in Yugoslavia and that they were assisted by Partisans.

A trio of "blackhanders" (I don't think the term needs any explanation in this image), led by a phlegmatic-looking Staff Sergeant (or maybe just tired; they all look tired), has just removed the #3 Pratt & Whitney R-1830-65 from this gray-painted PB-24L-FO, mount and all, as the designers had intended; the replacement will be nearby, waiting to be exchanged for this dud. The #3 was an important engine because it drove a propeller, and supplied power to the main hydraulic system pump. The aircraft is 44-48796, #78, of 767th BS, 461st BG, that arrived back in the US on June 16, 1945, for storage and salvage at Walnut Ridge.

A well-worn and oil-stained *Home For Christmas*, B-24H-15-FO 42-52437 has just released its bombs on a target in high summer 1944. Assigned to 778th BS, 464th BG, as E-Easy on March 9, 1944, it was transferred on February 15, 1945, to 459th BG, probably as a war-weary hack as it had been in combat almost a year by then. It was sent home on May 30 and designated as an RB-24 — another indicator of a war-weary aircraft — and the Reconstruction Finance Company accepted it at Altus, Oklahoma, on September 16.

A formation of 465th BG B-24s releases a rain of bombs on a target in Germany in summer 1944 among light flak. One aircraft, almost out of frame, at the top of the photograph, is already smoking from one engine, complicating (or worse) its return to base. In this image, it is easy to see the trajectory of the bombs as they arc forward at the release speed of the aircraft and not "straight down" as many imagine it.

Flak Strainer, B-24G 42-78289, appears not to have had to strain too much flak as it made it back to the US on April 29, 1945. Each time it returned to 825th BS, 484th BG, after servicing, it received a new battle number, #44 being its first, followed by #33 and finally #43. These numbers usually designated an aircraft's parking bay as well as identifying it in flight.

This art on B-24H-FO 42-52722 was never graced with text, but it was generally known as *Hell From Heaven*, which was used a number of times on various B-24s scattered across the globe. Received by the 15th AF on June 1, 1944, it was transferred shortly afterward to 830th BS, 485th BG, and was unfortunately to experience hell above Friedrichshafen on July 20, 1944. A few moments after the bombs were dropped, it received a direct flak hit in the bomb bay, which also punctured the fuel tanks and fire broke out. Within seconds, flames were coming out of the waist windows and the aircraft fell away until the tail separated and the remainder crashed in a tight spin in the target area. Four crew managed to exit the aircraft to become POWs, but the remainder were killed.

Another French Liberator order that was transferred to the RAF: Liberator II AL510, which operated into the Baltic states as part of the Special Operations Flight from Fayid, Egypt, coded as W-William. During the Battle of Alamein, the flight was taken off Special Operations and used to supplement the Liberators of 159 and 160 Squadrons. Later, it went to British Overseas Airlines Corporation (BOAC) as G-AHZP, then Scottish Aviation, which operated it on behalf of Iceland Airways. While flying in the Berlin Airlift, it undershot landing and crashed at Speke on October 13, 1948, while transporting milk.

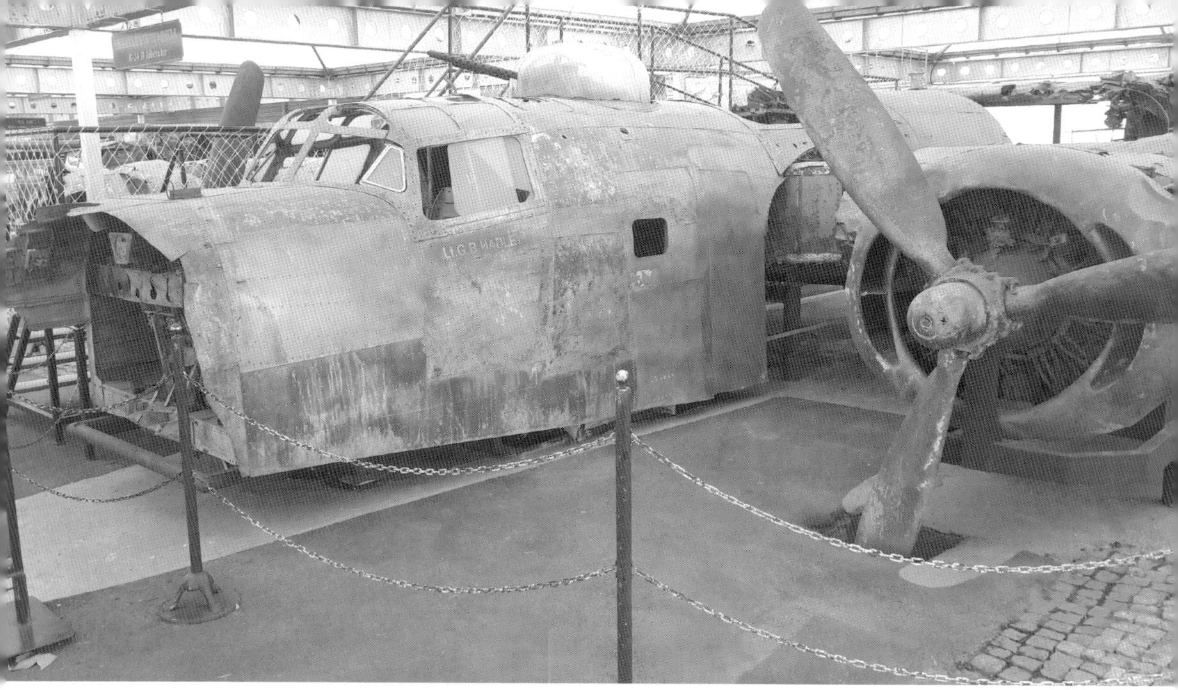

This photo, supplied by fellow B-24 historian Pavel Türk, shows the only existing ex-*Tidal Wave* airframe, B-24D 41-24311 *Hadley's Harem,* of 344th BS, 98th BG, as it is on display in the Rahmi M. Koç Museum, Istanbul. If you look closely at the nose, you will see a crude ring gunsight as this was one of the *Tidal Wave* aircraft fitted with fixed, forward-firing .50-calibre machine guns – in this instance, four of them. The aircraft was damaged over the target, and knowing that they could not make it back to Benghazi, Lt. Hadley's crew set course for Turkey, figuring that it was better than being made POW in Germany or Romania. They didn't quite make it, ditching just 750ft off the shoreline and three of the crew drowned.

Minnesota Marge was transferred to 376th BG by 15th AF and flew missions with 515th BS in April to June 1944. It went to the Gioia Depot for major overhaul and returned as a war-weary hack in September. The unit it was assigned to, on arrival in Italy, in December 1943, is not known, nor is the name it carried previously, *Old CXXXNE* acknowledged anywhere. It was salvaged at Gioia in August 1945.

Not a great deal is known about this aircraft. B-24J-CF 42-64363 *Li'l Butch* departed the US for 15th AF on March 9, 1944, but took until April 1 to reach Bari. Assigned to 718th BS, 449th BG as #27, it was flown mostly by the Henry Krawiec crew. Just why it was transferred to 376th BG on January 4, 1945, remains unknown, and the details of the combat damage that caused its salvage on February 22 are similarly unspecified.

The 450th BG arrived in Italy in late December 1943 and entered combat in January 1944; this is one of the original B-24s issued to the Group while working up in the US. Despite information suggesting it was abandoned by its crew and crashed into the sea, the reality is that 2/Lt Bernard J. Gillespie and crew in B-24H-FO 42-7740 *Big Blow Out* of 722nd BS returned to base on January 29, 1944, after a mission to bomb the Siena marshalling yard to find that the right main gear would not extend. The ensuing crash-landing ended with an over-run of the runway and hitting a stone wall; all crew were able to return to duty. At this early date, none of the Wing and Group markings seen in other 450th images in this book had been formalized, so it is a relatively "anonymous" looking aircraft.

This B-24J-CO, 44-40438, started combat duty with 8th AF in the UK, first assigned to 493rd BG in May 1944, then moving to 34th BG in June before storage at BAD 2, Warton, and transfer to 15th AF for assignment to 727th BS, 451st BG. Here, it is shown dropping 1,000lb bombs on a target just north of the Alps — possibly Salzburg. Note that the open waist window has a 15th AF-designed removable winter closure; it is way too far below zero at European bombing altitudes to be standing at an open window! The aircraft returned to the US on July 9, 1945, for storage and salvage.

B-24H-FO 42-52603 *Round Trip* of 736th BS, 454th BG, did not live up to its name this time — it did not even make the trip at all, crashing on take-off at San Giovanni on May 4, 1944, with Lt. Robert V. Batz in command. If the scoreboard under the pilot's window is up to date, it would have been its 14th mission. As can be seen from the photo, it did not "die" in vain, having been stripped of every conceivable useful item to keep other B-24s in the air. The missing plexiglass would probably have been used to make souvenir trinkets to send home to family and sweethearts.

The production line in the Consolidated Fort Worth, Texas, facility in late April 1944. On the right, B-24H-25-CFs assembled from Ford-manufactured parts are alternated with Fort Worth-assembled B-24J-50-CFs from Consolidated San Diego-manufactured parts, the latter in this case being British-order Liberator GR.VIs destined for the anti-submarine and shipping role in the RAF. On the left are C-87-CF transports 44-39214 to 44-39221, and in the far distance is the prototype Convair B-32 Dominator. In the foreground is 42-50395, which departed the US for 15th AF on May 26 to be assigned to 824th BS, 455th BG, #38, where it was named *Goona's Garbage Wagon*. Thirteen months later it was back in the US, its war complete.

42-64486, a B-24H-CF, arrived at Bari on January 8, 1944, to be assigned to 746th BS, 456th BG, #50, and named, not terribly originally, *The Piece-Maker*. By October, the 746th engineering staff deemed it no longer combat-worthy and it was consigned to Gioia as war-weary. The AAF was not finished with it, however. The depot spruced it up and 15th AF headquarters sent it to the 98th BG on February 9, 1945, where it flew two reconnaissance flights for the Group, one on February 25 and the other, on the last mission for the 98th in World War Two on April 15, with a period back at the depot in between those two flights. The next day, it returned to Gioia and was subsequently photographed in that unit's graveyard, never to return to the US.

A close-up of the "back end" of B-24L-FO 44-49789 *Linda Ann* of the 459th BG, showing its very recognizable checkered black-and-yellow tail identification markings. The rudder trim tab (on both rudders), originally only three ribs long, has been extended to five ribs in length. Note also the lightning "wick" to discharge the vertical stabilizer in the event of a strike. The tail turret is of interest, as it is the late-war so-called "lightweight turret," which was bereft of hydraulic power and the twin guns were hand-manipulated. The aircraft is showing its 758th BS assignment, the battle number #8F owing the 8 to the last number of the squadron. It arrived at the 459th on January 26, 1945, and by January 8, 1946, the Reconstruction Finance Company had it stored at Walnut Ridge.

In the pale 1945 autumn sun of Dübendorf, Switzerland, 42-52347 *Belle Ringer* of 763rd BS, 460th BG, K-King runs up its engines on the grass where it has been interned since June 13, 1944, preparatory to being able to fly to the UK. Originally with the 762nd BS, coded R-Roger, it had transferred to the 763rd BS when, on the Munich mission of that date, the aircraft was seen to experience mechanical problems with #1 engine, which was then shut down. When last seen, it appeared to be intending to fly to the target and drop its bombs. Unfortunately, on September 27, 1945, during its return to the UK, it ran out of fuel and crashed near Paris.

Stopping over again at Rufisque, Dakar, for fuel, and no doubt heading in the opposite direction this time, is gray-painted PB-24L 44-49242 of 764th BS, 461st BG, #19. The aircraft was subject to a MACR on January 19, 1945, after a flak hit over the target (Brod, Yugoslavia) caused a fire in the nose and the navigator and bombardier baled out and were captured. The fire was successfully extinguished, and the aircraft returned to base. Retained in Italy for some time post-war, it was declared excess in October 1945 and was back in the US on November 4, for Reconstruction Finance Company storage at Walnut Ridge, Arkansas.

Arriving at 777th BS, 464th BG, in March 1944, B-24H-FO 42-52487 *Lucky* Strike, Q-Queen, was damaged by flak over Wiener Neustadt on July 16, 1944, and crash-landed at Foggia on return. An RAF Baltimore can be seen at the left.

A close-up look at B-24H-FO 42-52456, A-Able, named *Memories*. On the Ploești mission of June 6, 1944, it was shot down by flak. A witness observed "Lt. Funk's [2/Lt. Glenferd E. Funk] ship was flying along normally about three miles north of Bucharest..." when it was struck by flak between #2 engine and the fuselage and burst into flames. Lt. Funk pulled the aircraft out of formation and the crew baled out before the aircraft fell into a flat spin all the way to the ground. All crew landed safely and became POWs, returning to the US in September.

B-24H-FO 42-52632 Flaming Mamie, #55, of 826th BS, 484th BG, basks in the sun at Torretta airfield. On August 22, 1944, during a mission to a target in Austria, the formation was attacked by Fw-190s, setting either #3 or #4 engine on fire (reports vary). The aircraft initially dropped away to the left and then banked right to begin a turn for home and slid away from the formation, but the wolves knew a crippled aircraft was easy meat and set upon it. Five parachutes were seen before the aircraft exploded. All ten escaped, however, landing in Hungary and were taken POW.

Yet another B-24H-FO, 42-52592 *High Hopes* started out as original equipment of 487th BG, 839th BS (8th AF), coded R5-J, before going into storage with BAD 3 when 487th BG switched to the B-17. The art was sourced from an Auto-Lite spark plug magazine advertisement. On January 10, 1945, it was transferred to 15th AF and is first noted at 829th BS 485th BG, on February 7, coded L-Love. After hostilities ceased, it was sent to Gioia for assessment on May 16. It passed its POM inspection, returned to the US and ended its days with the RFC at Altus, Oklahoma.

B-24D 42-40654 *Kate Smith* was originally slated for Operation *Tidal Wave* as part of the 345th BS, 98th BG, but on July 29, 1943, while being test-flown by a 389th BG pilot, it crash-landed at Benina, Libya. The Kate Smith the aircraft was named for was referred to as The First Lady of Radio, well known for her renditions of Irving Berlin's *God Bless America* and *When the Moon Comes Over the Mountain*, the latter being referenced by the art. Despite the Category 4 damage being repaired, it was not flown on missions by the 98th, and when this photograph was taken on November 1 it was being overhauled by 43rd Service Group at Benghazi. By December 1944, it was graded war weary and at Gioia, where it was salvaged, on April 28, 1945.

Originally delivered to 514th BS, 376th BG, at Palestine, B-24D 41-23660 became *Poison Ivy*, #53, in September 1942. Almost immediately (on October 7), it was directed to 7th BG on temporary duty and flown to Allahabad, India, thence to Dinjan (India), Kunming (China) and finally to Hsinghing. On October 21, the crew successfully bombed the Lingsi coal mine's facility on a mission lasting 12–14 hours. It later returned to North Africa and flew its first mission from Palestine on November 11, 1942. On January 31, 1943, the 376th attacked Messina but were badly mauled by Me-109s, and despite losing two engines and with more than 700 holes in the aircraft, the Stewart crew made it to Malta and crash-landed there. The last time they saw the aircraft it was being pushed into a quarry by the RAF.

There were approximately 20 B-24s that carried this name in various forms including stardust, star dust and starduster. This particular *Star Dust*, B-24H-FO 42-52188, was original equipment of 737th BS, 454th BG, assigned in the US on December 2, 1943. After summer 1944, it was often photographed as it was used as a static training aircraft before being returned to combat, initially as the aircraft of the "Spider" Webb crew, later the Morris crew. It passed to 513th BS, 376th BG, in January 1945 as #26, and in February to 718th BS, 449th BG, as war-weary, retaining #26 on the nose but #30 on the tail. It was salvaged at Gioia post-war, recorded as August 1945, but probably earlier.

Another popular name was *Bottoms Up*. This B-24H-CF, 42-64448, flew with 721st BS, 450th BG, as #27. Original equipment of the 450th, it arrived in Italy with the Group in January 1944. It flew more than 100 missions before being declared war-weary on November 14, 1944, but remained on strength as a transport aircraft. It was apparently pressed into service on the occasional mission as it was lost in unknown circumstances during the March 16, 1945, mission to the Wiener Neustadt rail marshalling yards. Outbound, while still on climb over the Adriatic, the formation passed through heavy cloud and when clear of the cloud: #27 never rejoined the formation. Nothing was ever found of the aircraft, and it assumed to have ditched or crashed in the ocean. All nine aboard were declared dead one year after the loss date.

Despite the fires lit to obscure the target, one of the Ploești refineries' tank farms is burning strongly. Above is B-24J-CO 44-40196, *Weesie* #16, of 727th BS, 451st BG. On August 23, 1944, the aircraft was in the vicinity of Wiener Neustadt with Markersdorf as the target when it was shot down. The details are sketchy because the original MACR is missing and there are only the recollections of some of the crew some years later. There was a large fire in the bomb bay probably caused by a direct flak hit, which caused the aircraft to explode fairly quickly, and while most seem to have baled out, at least two were unaccounted for.

An excellent image of a nose wheel collapse, showing details of the early model B-24G, particularly the twin braces on the pitot, an identifying feature of all B-24Gs. *Shack-Up*, 42-78080 of 736th BS, 454th BG, suffered a landing accident on March 2, 1944, which caused the nose wheel to fold. It was repaired and flew missions until November when it was reduced to war-weary status. On January 20, 1945, it was selected for detached service with the RAF. In all, a dozen Liberators of various models, mainly B-24Gs, were taken on charge by Mediterranean Allied Air Forces, designated as B.Mk.VI with serials TW758—TW769 and transferred for special duties including agent dropping, etc. All were converted with nose turrets removed and parachute hatches and slides installed, and all but two were returned to the USAAF after the war.

A scene repeated often at airfields around the globe, in this case San Giovanni, home of the 455th BG. 741st BS B-24J-CO 44-40517 *Irish Lassie,* #20, has been met by an ambulance to remove the body of a crew member killed by fighter attack during a bombing mission. 20mm explosive shell damage can be seen aft of the waist hatch and further damage is visible on the wing. Other men, probably the crew, cluster together and examine other damage suffered in the attack. The aircraft was repaired and returned to the US in late June 1945.

Despite the obvious connotations with this name, and the number of orders from senior officers who demanded such names be removed, there was a surprising number of B-24s that carried it. The photo shows B-24H-CF 42-64489 *Purple Shaft*, #48, of 746th BS, 456th BG. It was struck in the waist area by either a cannon shell or flak round, which did not explode during the June 13, 1944, mission. By February 1945, it was deemed war-weary and transferred to 725th BS, 451st BG, where it was renamed *Much Wampum*. On April 25, it was buzzing the Island of Capri, hit a lighthouse and crashed into the sea. The three crew and two civilian passengers were killed.

B-24H-FO 42-52339 was *Little Butch*, #9X, of 759th BS, 459th BG, proven by the four-leaf clover prominent on the nose. It departed the US for Italy on January 20, 1944, under the command of 1/Lt. Robert W. Spargur. By the end of 1944, it was regarded as war weary and received by 723rd BS, 450th BG, where it suffered an accident and was written off on March 3, 1945.

It looks as if *Mexicali Rose* has begun a process of having the underside painted black and that someone got a bit carried away with the pre-painting cleaning fluid, stripping off part of the name. B-24J-CO 44-40514 of 762nd BS, 460th BG, C-Charlie, tucks in close to the photographic aircraft with bomb bay doors open. It transferred to 763rd BS where it was renamed *Coke Hi* and shot down by flak on Christmas Day, 1944, on a mission to Graz, Austria, with a 760th BS crew. It was observed to be struck between engines #3 and #4. It left the formation but remained under control initially before commencing a steep dive, which became a spin before exploding. No parachutes were observed against the snow background, but five of the crew did survive.

Seen here on a summer 1944 mission is B-24H-FO 42-52398 *Boise Belle* of 766th BS, 461st BG, #41, its early 15th AF markings "bleeding through" the final style. After 11 months of combat, it became war weary and while in storage at Gioia it was salvaged on March 24, 1945.

Known as *Oswald the Rabbit* but carrying only the art, B-24H-FO 42-95374, L-Love, tucks in close to the photographer. Flying with 777th BS, 464th BG, for less than three months, it was written off in a crash-landing at Pantanella on August 21, 1944.

In the foreground of this flight of 781st BS, 465th BG, B-24s is B-24L-FO 44-49380 *Skin Wagon,* J-Jig. It appears to have suffered damage to the left vertical stabilizer, as the replacement has come from a camouflaged aircraft in the boneyard. It also has no group markings on the right stabilizer. The name is another euphemism. It was delivered to the Group on December 21, 1944, and left the Group for Gioia on May 25, 1945, returning to the US to be stored by the RFC at Walnut Ridge, Arkansas.

At times, aircraft get their nicknames from the most obscure of sources. The pilot of *Fuel-Cell Fanny* explains this one: "The plane named herself. We had to change fuel cells three times before getting one that didn't leak. Each crew member had his wife's name painted beside his station. My wife's name was Madelene." *Fanny* was B-24H-CF 41-29502, 824th BS, 484th BG, #12, and was a victim of the wholesale replacement of older aircraft by the 15th AF in December 1944. Once the flow of replacements had increased; it was downgraded to war-weary and was salvaged at Gioia on April 17, 1945.

A nice study of in-flight B-24H-CF 41-29536 *Ring Dang Doo!* of 830th BS, 485th BG, Q-Queen. It is first traced in the Group on July 7, 1944, and appears on the formation chart for the Group's last mission of April 25, 1945. On return from one mission, it made a diversion to Vis for fuel or maintenance before returning to its base at Venosa. War over, it was sent to Gioia on May 16, assessed as war-weary in June and salvaged on July 30.

One of the more famous photographs taken of the war in the air 1939—45 but not necessarily fully captioned or correctly attributed. This is the death throes of PB-24L-FO 44-49710 *Stevonovitch II*, 776th BS, 464th BG, N-Nan, and the photograph was taken by radio/gunner Leland Conrad from the right waist of Q-Queen. On April 10, 1945, while attacking tactical targets around Lugo in Northern Italy, the aircraft was hit by flak just behind the #1 engine (all reports say #4, but the photo clearly shows the left wing) and that portion of the wing immediately broke off, snapping the aircraft into a left roll and subsequent spin. The pilot was Lt. Col. James H. Gilson and the only survivor, standing in the bomb bay at the time and flung out by the snap roll, was 1/Lt. Edward F. Walsh, the radar navigator.

With the name *Kickapoo* it seems likely that there were some Texans among this crew. B-24D 41-11768 was assigned to 344th BS, 98th BG, in time to take part in Operation *Tidal Wave*. There is some mystery about it, however, as it departed the US for North Africa on August 1, 1942, not arriving until September 18. Just where it was and what it was doing before July 31, 1943, cannot be established, but since 41-11767 *Shanghai Lil* flew with the 98th from August 1942, *Kickapoo* must have done also but its records are missing. It was not to end well, however, as *Kickapoo* was the first loss of the mission. On take-off, #4 engine failed, the aircraft staggered around for a return landing, dumping its bombs in the Mediterranean, struck a concrete power pole, crashed and exploded. Only two burned men struggled from the wreckage and survived.

Not a great deal is known about B-24D 42-72765 *Sexy Sal*. It departed the US for North Africa on September 6, 1942, and was assigned to 514th BS, 376th BG, as #64. It returned to the US on July 18, 1944, without any explanation, so it has been assumed that ten months of combat wore it out. There is a photograph of a B-24 #765 as a radio-controlled target aircraft "mother ship," which was thought to be this aircraft, re-assigned on return to the US, but that has now been identified as 42-63765.

The aircraft in the 95-degree right bank in this photograph is obviously in distress. B-24H-FO 42-52096 *Marty the Rubble Maker* of 722nd BS, 450th BG, was part of the mission to Porto Santo Stefano on the west coast of Italy, its first mission, when a flak burst blew off the majority of the left vertical stabilizer as it left the target. 2/Lt. J.C. Word managed to hold formation for about four minutes while the crew baled out before losing control, the aircraft doing a "split S" a number of times before diving into the Mediterranean. The body of one man was recovered, to be determined killed in action, while the rest were declared dead after a lapse of time.

There is film of this crash landing, no doubt available online, but this is a well captured moment near the end of the slide. The aircraft is *Miss Fury*, B-24H-CF 41-29212, #22, of 721st BS, 450th BG, one of the original aircraft assigned to the Group in the US, prior to deployment. For the cameramen to be in position to record the landing, an undercarriage problem had to have been known about in advance. The left main collapsed and the aircraft slid to a halt in a cloud of dust on March 13, 1944, at Manduria and was written off five days later. Miss Fury was a 1941 cartoon superhero, and the first to be written and drawn by a woman.

After having made mention of 15th AF's Advanced Depot 52 Gioia del Colle many times, I thought it reasonable to show a photo of the place where so many of these B-24s spent at least some time in maintenance, were salvaged or sent back to the US to take their battle-hardened crews home. Originally, it was an Italian AFB and is so today, but it was captured by the British 8th Army in October 1943, repaired and put into service as a USAAF depot. It was also home for short periods in 1944 to the 451st BG and the 464th BG while their permanent bases were completed. It was returned to the Italian military in September 1945.

Other books you might like:

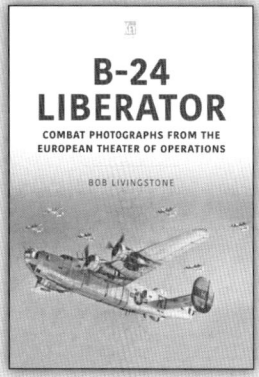

Historic Military Aircraft Series, Vol. 21

Historic Military Aircraft Series, Vol. 11

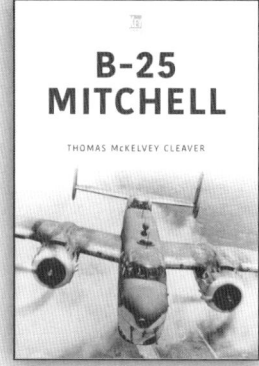

Historic Military Aircraft Series, Vol. 12

Historic Military Aircraft Series, Vol. 30

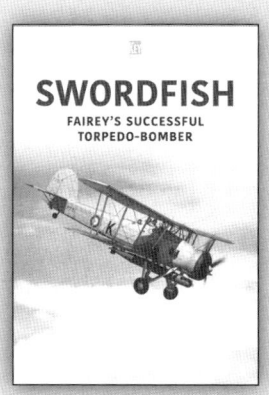

Historic Military Aircraft Series, Vol. 28

Historic Military Aircraft Series, Vol. 31

For our full range of titles please visit:
shop.keypublishing.com/books

VIP Book Club

Sign up today and receive
TWO FREE E-BOOKS

Be the first to find out about our forthcoming book releases and receive exclusive offers.

Register now at **keypublishing.com/vip-book-club**

Our VIP Book Club is a 100% spam-free zone, and we will never share your email with anyone else. You can read our full privacy policy at: privacy.keypublishing.com